GOOSE

IMAGINE THE POSSIBILITIES

FREDERICK W. PENNEY

Quantity sales special discounts are available on quantity purchases by corporations, associations, and others. For details, contact the publisher at carol@markvictorhansenlibrary.com

Orders by U.S. trade bookstores and wholesalers.
Email: carol@markvictorhansenlibrary.com

Creative contribution by Walker Kornfeld
Cover Design - Low & Joe Creative, Brea, CA 92821
Illustrations - Bob Eckstein
Book Layout - DBree, StoneBear Design

Manufactured and printed in the United States of America distributed globally by markvictorhansenlibrary.com

New York | Los Angeles | London | Sydney

ISBN: 979-8-88581-029-6 Hardback
ISBN: 979-8-88581-030-2 Paperback
ISBN: 979-8-88581-031-9 eBook
Library of Congress Control Number: 2022907987

CONTENTS

PROLOGUE

There are times in your life when you just know that the next phase of your life and thought process will take a slight turn. A year ago, I was prompted to start thinking about writing a book about *my* life and decades of hard work, failures (which are only experiences), and success. Having grown up in a small Northern California farm town in the 1970's I learned a lot of life lessons and learned the importance of work and surviving on very little money. We were not broke, of course. We had a very conscientious mother and father who worked their fingers to the bone to try and put food on the table for four rambunctious growing boys. These lessons are taught indirectly through the characters portrayed in the Goose novel, taking you ahead of where I am now in my life and yet jumping back to where I was before any personal and financial success occurred.

This is the first book in a series of three. The second book takes us back to my childhood. And the third, well, you'll just have to wait and see.

I have learned that nothing comes easy in life and that those who pursue their dreams relentlessly and with passion and fervor, good things will always win out over the bad. Don't get me wrong—there will be failures along the way and life lessons that may not be so pleasant, but they are valuable lessons indeed, and if you take them in the right vein and just keep getting off the ground your success will be sweet.

Mind me, success does not mean being rich as that is a relative term because we are all on a different plain in life. I truly believed I was well off when I was growing up on our small gentleman's ranch in rural Northern California. But I did not know any better and as such there was nothing telling me that I did not have much money. Everyone around me was in the same boat and so we enjoyed life to its fullest.

I always tell people other than the family that has now grown, I am no happier now in life than I was in the 1970's. Other than my family my joy is no greater now than when I was broke while growing up. I loved my early life and sometimes go back to that time and place to help me realize what is truly important in life—family, God, country, and friends. In fact, until recently I had a mailbox at the post office in that small town where I grew up. It gave me a reason to drive down the old country roads that I so fondly remember, stop at the post office and open my P.O. Box filled to the brim with junk mail. Yes, the heads turn when the fancy European luxury car glides up and down those roads at a slow pace helping me reflect on why I have been so blessed and why God put me here on this earth help my family and others live their dreams.

I do know that with the help of others, writing this book has been a joy to walk down memory lane and remember the wonderful times spent with family and friends. Through characters, important life lessons can be learned and applied in your life to help you navigate the rough waters of life and succeed as I have. This is my goal and dream—to inspire others to never give up and know that most of the time becoming successful in all ways takes time, patience, and a lot of perseverance.

Enjoy! For it is not every day that I open my life to others

CHAPTER

1

The helicopter thundered in my ears despite the headset, rattling me in my seat as I gazed out the window. Shielding my eyes from the late-morning sun, the lush Northern California greenery stretched on for miles, interrupted only by the sprawling Collins estate and its man-made lake.

"Circle the grounds first, Tony," I told the pilot. "I want to see how everything looks from above."

His voice crackled through my headset. "Yes ma'am." Holding us steady at about eight hundred feet, he veered toward the western edge of the property. Acres of manicured lawn dotted with pines, oaks, and hemlocks surrounded the main house and its many out-buildings, interspersed with colorful gardens and stone pathways that snaked through the rolling landscape. Three guesthouses dotted the sparse woods to the west, the aquamarine of their swimming pools contrasting the surrounding greenery and dark tiles of the rooftops.

Tennis and basketball courts lay to the north, near a driving range and putting green. Beyond those, a flat expanse contained an oval dirt go-kart track with a barn and a long row of tiered bleachers. A packed-gravel parking lot connected a narrow dirt road that wound its way through various outbuildings and past the main guesthouse to the northeast. The road turned to pavement and continued east, unfurling like a ribbon through fields of grazing cows on its way to I-80 and Lake Tahoe, about an hour distant.

I turned my attention to the main house at the center of it all. A contemporary take on Victorian architecture, the sprawl of its peaked rooftops dwarfed all other structures. The gallery and auditorium were to the north, adjacent to the swimming pool and sauna. The garages sat to the west, acting as both museum and showroom, in addition to their traditional purpose. A brick plaza sprawled the grounds to the east, lined with towering hedges and a long garden running through its center, leading up to the main entrance. A massive formation of granite rocks welcomed visitors near the entrance.

Though too far to see from this distance, I knew well what lay etched in their surface—the Collins family crest—consisting of a shield bearing a cross between two stylized lions, all beneath a crown and laurels—and the extensive Collins family tree, going back generations. The dark blue of the lake shimmered to the south, lined with a boathouse, docks, and picnic areas. From the water's edge to the house, a large stretch of grass led uphill to an open series of stone steps bifurcating wide, tiered verandas, each dotted with dozens of small, round tables set up for the occasion. Nearly everywhere, I could see staff and delivery vehicles bustling about, creating a flurry of activity.

My ears popped as the pilot descended to the helipad near the northwestern edge of the lake. My assistant, a young woman dressed in business casual, stood clear as we touched down. Clutching a leather-bound tablet, she raised a hand to a small ear-mounted headset and mic, holding it in place against the buffeting wind of the rotors.

"Thanks, Tony," I said, gathering my things. "Grab a bite from the kitchen if you like but be ready to go in case we need you."

"Will do. Thanks ma'am," he replied, flicking switches and checking gauges.

The roar of the rotors and descending whine of the engine assaulted my ears as I removed the headset. I hung it up before opening the door. Grabbing my messenger bag, I scurried clear in a crouch.

"How are we looking, Emily?" I shouted.

"Good," she yelled back, handing me her tablet as we made for the house. "Thomas and the footmen have all the tables set up. Food deliveries are on schedule. Chef Eliot has the kitchens in full swing. Mable is briefing the special event staff. They'll have table linens and decorations completed in a few hours. The school bus is due at one o'clock, and Eddie brought on a few local mechanics to help prepare. They're at the track now. Most of the family is here, with the rest arriving before the race. The pyrotechnicians will be here this afternoon to set up the fireworks—I can't believe William was able to get us a permit, by the way—and the string quartet is due at four." She stopped to take a break and looked at me. "But there's an issue with the main walk-in cooler. It looks like a compressor issue."

"Has Ralph taken a look?"

She continued. "Yes, I'm waiting for an update, but he seemed doubtful. He may have to have parts delivered. He can likely have it up and running before this evening, but chef is going to have a dozen banquet carts of hors d'oeuvres ready over the next few hours, some served cold, some hot—to say nothing of the rest of what's stored in the cooler."

I flicked a finger around the screen of the tablet, skimming the various notes and schedules. "Okay. Let's prepare as if the cooler will be down permanently. There's an extensive basement with plenty of storage. It's in the low fifties down there. See what Eddie can do to drop the temperature to thirty-eight degrees. Tell chef to use the north service elevator but check the dimensions first. It may be quicker and easier to transfer the food onto proofing racks before moving them. There should be more racks in storage if needed. For ingredients and other stored items, divvy up what you can into the remaining coolers and move the rest to the basement. Update Thomas on the situation. Pull four servers and four footmen to assist. Once the heavy lifting is done and everything's under control, have two servers remain with chef to act as runners for the evening. Alert Mable that she'll be down two servers for a while and tell her to let me know if she has any problems."

"You got it," Emily replied, tapping notes into her phone.

"What else?" I asked, handing her the tablet.

"We have two more requests for landings. A senator and a businesswoman of a successful Bay Area tech company. The rest of the guests are confirmed by car."

"Okay. Get with Marcus in security. He'll confirm them and coordinate with their pilots. Make sure Thomas has assigned a valet to cover the helipad. What's the head count?"

"Two hundred and forty-seven." She shrugged.

I laughed. "Over two dozen more than expected. Why do plus-ones always turn into plus-twos and threes?"

"An overly generous host would be my guess."

"Absolutely." I shook my head. "What else?"

"Your dress arrived. It's waiting in your guest room. And the quartet will want to see you after they've set up to go over the music. You may wish to check in with chef. You know how he gets. And Mable would like a few minutes to go over the selection of sparkling cider and juice. Also, just to confirm, can we review the alcohol policy again?"

I laughed. "You already know the answer to that. William and his wife Helen don't drink. Nor do they provide alcohol at any of their events. However, they turn a blind eye to those who bring their own. It's a running joke—guests pretend they haven't smuggled in any contraband, and William pretends he doesn't see it. If any of the guests ask the servers for an alcoholic drink, the servers should politely explain that this is a dry event."

"Gotcha," Emily said. "I'll make sure everyone understands."

We made our way up the stone steps, stopping at the highest tier just before the entrance to the house. A crew busied themselves setting up a dais and PA system. "Well done, Emily. Any better and they wouldn't need me at all."

"Thanks," she replied, beaming. "You only turn seventy-five once, right?"

"That's right, it's a big day. Speaking of, where is the birthday boy?"

She gave a nervous laugh. "We, uh, we lost track of him. Helen hasn't seen him. I have people checking the barn. We thought maybe he was tinkering with his tractors."

I snickered. "Always full of surprises. It's okay, call

off the search. I know where he is. Helen knows too, but she's as mischievous as he is."

"Oh, good." She tapped her earpiece and adjusted her mic. "Adrienne, crisis averted. Gather everyone and head back to Mable."

"I'll see you in an hour or two," I said. "Call or text if you need me."

"Sounds good. The first guests are due to arrive at six. We'll need the helipad clear by then."

"Got it. See you in a bit. Let Helen know I'll have him back shortly." As Emily headed inside, I set out across the veranda to the tree line at the far eastern edge of the lake.

***

Almost a mile from the house, past the main grounds and into the forest, I kept the water's edge on my right as I walked a faint dirt path through the trees. Before long, an expansive clearing appeared, giving a fine view of the placid water. A few dozen Fay Elberta peach trees stood in orderly rows—William's favorite. Their thick lower limbs gave way to thinner branches laden with yellow-orange peaches amongst thin green leaves.

Nearest the water stood an especially large tree, its branches sprawling almost horizontally from its thick trunk, creating an impressive canopy. From the largest of its lower branches hung a swing, and upon it sat William Collins.

"Meredith!" he called. "My favorite law partner, business partner, and organizer of festivities." He sprung from his seat with a step that belied his silver hair and wrinkled features. "You're late!"

I laughed, reaching up for a hug as we traded kisses on each cheek. "I had to spend half the day searching for an old fool who got himself lost," I retorted, brushing some stray leaves from his broad shoulders. "Have you seen him?"

"Well," he said, "more fool me for doubting you. Should I find him, you'll be the first to know."

"Happy birthday, William."

"Thank you, my dear. How go the preparations?"

"Everything's in hand. There's an issue with the kitchen walk-in, but we figured it out. I've got to make some rounds before the guests start arriving, but there's plenty of time."

He resumed his seat on the swing. "Thank you for coordinating everything, though I don't know why you bother. There are half a dozen people off the top of my head who could have handled it."

"My assistant Emily included," I replied, "but you know me. I prefer to be hands-on. Besides, no one knows the guest list better than I do."

"Quite right. Oh, there may be a few more than expected."

"Yes, I noticed. If there are any more, we'll have to open up the north wing."

"Now there's an idea," he mused.

I laughed. "Mable would have a fit. She'd want to clean every square inch—again—and she'd want more decorations besides."

"Yes, I suppose you're right."

I studied him as his sharp eyes gazed across the water, a large hand picking at one of the ropes of the swing. "Why'd you go AWOL, William? Is the anticipation getting to you? Wondering if you'll get that new tractor you've always wanted?"

"Ha! I should be so lucky." He stood, moving to a low-hanging branch. "How are you today, my lovelies?" he said, inspecting a cluster of fruit. "Getting enough sunshine? Almost ready for the harvest?" He picked two large peaches, tossing me one, then pointed to the swing. "This is the best seat on the estate. I like to come here to think. You know how I am about my solitude."

I rolled the firm peach around in my hands. A golden yellow with shots of red, it was nearly ripe to perfection. "What's on your mind?"

Sitting back down, he studied his peach, shaking his head. "For once, I don't know, my dear." He pointed to the canopy above us. "I grafted this tree from the farm I grew up on. I had one just like it as a kid—a giant Fay Elberta, swing and all." He gestured to the other trees. "All of these are either descendants of my farm or the neighboring farms I worked on as a teenager. Up until my family moved away, I made many important decisions on that swing. Almost thirty years ago, some twenty-five years after Helen and I broke ground on the house, I asked the family living on the old farm if I could take a graft of one of their trees. And for the past several years, I've sat in this swing." He rubbed a thumb along the rope, his eyes returning to the water. "Looking at the world from the opposite end of life is a bit surreal, I must say."

"But a long and fruitful life it's been," I offered.

William laughed, pretending to throw his peach at me. "Blast you and your puns." He rose from his seat again, his movements frustrated, full of pent-up energy. "The older I get, the more convinced I become that I haven't done enough. There's still more to do, I just don't know what."

"Oh, I see."

"Do you?"

"You're in between projects again, aren't you?"

He paused, releasing a defeated sigh. "Yes, I certainly am. The past year establishing new partnerships to secure rare computing elements for various ventures has been an amazing challenge, and a lucrative one. Thank you for your help with that, by the way. But I'm ready for something new. Something unlike anything I've done before."

"That's a tall order. You've done more than anyone I know."

"Perhaps," he muttered.

I took a bite from my peach. "I may have something for you, but I need a little more time."

He perked up, his eyes coming alight. "Oh, really? What is it?"

"I can't say, not yet. But it might just make the perfect birthday present."

"Wonderful! I certainly don't need extravagant gifts. Between Helen, the kids, the grandkids, and you of course, I have everything I could ever want. But if it's a new business venture or project of some kind, I'd be most interested." He clapped his hands, rubbing them together. "Well, we should be getting back. I want to be at the go-kart track before the kids arrive."

"Go on ahead," I said. "I'll catch up in a minute."

"Don't be long," he replied, starting down the dirt path. "This old fool might get lost again!"

I walked deeper into the grove, inspecting the trees. Though smaller and younger than William's favorite, they appeared in good health. Heavy with fruit, they would be harvested in a few weeks. Chef Eliot would have his hands full preserving them, but a good portion of the harvest would go to local elementary schools. The Collins family recipes for peach cobbler and sliced peaches with milk and sugar for breakfast had become local favorites.

Three trees toward the back of the grove stood out,

their branches lighter, their fruit small and sickly. Running a hand through the leaves, I found spots of varying color dotting their skin. I checked the surrounding trees while scrolling through the contacts on my phone. I called Victor, the founder of FRD, a research and development firm based in Texas.

"Hey, Victor. You won't believe this."

"What's up?"

"The trees at the estate need to be tested, too."

"You're kidding."

"Nope. I don't understand it. It's such a small grove."

"Whoever William has tending it likely plays a part," Victor replied. "Contaminated equipment."

"I'll ask the groundskeeper. Maybe some of his staff moonlights at other orchards."

"Good idea. Get a list of locations. We'll fold this local outbreak into our wider plans." A muffled PA announcement sounded in the background. "I just landed in Sacramento Meredith. I have some work to finish up, but I'll be there around eight or so."

"Great. See you tonight."

CHAPTER
2

"**V**im! Vigor!" William's shouts carried across the go-kart track, having no effect on the two yellow labs careening across the grounds. More white than yellow, they chased birds with abandon. "Would someone corral those two? We need a border collie. Do Border Collies herd other dogs?"

"I got it, Dad," Maggie said, letting out a loud whistle. The dogs froze, ears perked, before setting off at a sprint toward us. The family had gathered in front of the long bleachers set before the track's main straightaway. Footmen were busy setting up several long tables end-to-end, while servers unloaded snacks and drinks from the nearby golf carts and utility vehicles.

Most of the family members confirmed they were coming. William and Helen's daughter Maggie, with her husband Greg, helped the staff unfurl linens over the tables and set up refreshments. Their sons, Scott and Eric, sat on the bleachers with their wives.

"Never mind the dogs, William," Helen scolded from the bleachers. "Come say hello to your grandchildren."

William turned to his son, William Jr. "Bill, will you find the leashes? Eddie's about to send a few of our young drivers out to test the karts. I don't want the dogs to cause an accident."

The spitting image of his father from twenty years ago, Bill hopped off the bleachers. At six-foot-four with a swimmer's body and blonde hair, his blue eyes shone brighter than his smile. "You got it, Pop."

"Check that utility vehicle," Bill's wife Alice pointed. "I think I saw them in the back." She sat with their children, Emma and Jason. Emma cradled an infant daughter, William's only great-grandchild—so far.

A few close family friends, along with various other family members from Helen's side, made up the rest of the gathering, including two sisters with their husbands, children, and grandchildren. Some of the kids were barely old enough to walk, while others romped around with Vim and Vigor, sneaking them snacks under the tables.

William walked arm-in-arm with Helen, visiting their great-grandchild as they caught up with the goings-on of their grandchildren. Most in their mid-twenties, William was always eager to learn of their budding careers. It was rare to have the whole family together in one place, and he was quick with advice and recommendations.

"Remember!" William nearly shouted at his grandson, Jason. "Resist, resist, resist." The family broke into laughter as he looked about in surprise. "What? Oh. Have I proffered that advice before?"

"Only all the time, Grandad," Jason said. "Along

with the marriage advice. 'Marry a solution, not a problem. That's why I married your grandmother.'"

William threw his arms wide. "Well, I admit I may have handed out these nuggets of truth a time or two in the past." He raised a finger, unable to help himself. "But it's true. Especially so early on. You've yet to graduate law school. And though you likely have a place waiting for you at my firm or your father's, now is not the time for lavish spending."

Jason sighed. "I know, Grandad, I know. But this boat is a really good deal. I've had my eye on something like it for a while."

William shook his head. "Such deals will still be around in five or ten years. And just imagine the position you'll be in by then. Deals down the road will pale in comparison to this one, as will your future boat in comparison to whatever dinghy you're considering today. Resisting that urge is how you secure your future, my boy." He turned to his kids, looking for backup. "Maggie, Bill, what did I advise over twenty years ago, when you left Collins and Associates to establish your own firm? You were both wildly successful personal injury attorneys at the family firm, and you brought an impressive list of clients to your new practice. You began building on that list immediately, then opening what? Two satellite offices in the Bay Area within the first year? And still, what did I advise?"

Maggie and Bill exchanged a look. "Gee, Dad," Maggie said, wide-eyed. "I don't seem to recall."

"Wait," Bill added, squinting at the sky. "Wasn't it something about relinquishing? Relegating? I think it was an R-word."

"Reestablishing!" Maggie exclaimed.

"Yup," Bill said, pointing at her, "that's it exactly. Reestablish."

William looked on in shock as the family laughed. "Who are you, and what have you done with my children?"

"We remember, Dad," Maggie smiled, glancing at Bill.

"'Resist, resist, resist,'" they said as one.

William swept a hand toward them, displaying his evidence to Jason. "You see there? Just like the many times I had to resist, resist, resist disciplining your wayward father."

Jason picked at his plastic cup of lemonade, laughing. "Okay, Grandad, I got it." He looked to his parents. "I seem to recall hearing much the same, growing up."

William beamed at the news. "Well, that's very good to hear. It appears I got through to them after all."

Bill's daughter Emma rocked her baby in her arms. "Trust me, Grandad. I think I speak for all of us kids when I say we grew up hearing those words."

"I'm very glad to hear that," William said. "It goes

double for you and your husband Kevin. His young career in the NFL is a tremendous accomplishment, but his profession is far more precarious than others."

Emma nodded. "We've talked about it a lot. He's always been interested in the coaching side of the game, so he's already preparing for a career in that direction once his playing days are over."

"Smart thinking," William agreed. "Always be looking five to ten years down the road. That kind of foresight will give you the direction you need to avoid many unpleasant surprises."

Maggie smiled at me. "I bet Meredith received many of these same lectures, growing up."

I nodded. "Oh, yes. My mother first gave me the resist advice when I was fourteen. I'd made a good chunk of money tutoring, and I wanted to go on a ski trip with some friends. She convinced me to keep building my savings. By the time I was sixteen, I was able to buy my first car—with plenty left over to keep building upon."

"And that advice never expires either," Maggie said. "About two years after Bill and I started our firm, we filed a major class action suit that would either ruin us or establish our position as one of California's top personal injury firms." She turned to Scott and Eric. "You two were in middle school back then. Uncertainties like that one are why we stayed in that tract house in Sacramento until you hit high school, well after we won the case."

Her husband Greg chimed in. "And here's the main thing. If the firm had suffered a loss, we would have been fine, financially. I can't tell you what a difference that knowledge made during the years that case dragged on. Your mother and I resisted the urge to spend the way we could have, instead investing heavily in our future. Success isn't meant to be squandered. It's meant to help you ensure that you and your family will be taken care of, no matter what happens."

"Here, here!" William raised his fist in the air.

"Alright, Grandad," Jason conceded. "I won't buy the boat. I'll sock the money away or invest it, how's that?"

"Ah, investments. Come with me," William replied, waving Jason over as he grabbed the leashes from Bill. William put a hand on Jason's shoulder as they headed up the grassy lane between the bleachers and the waist-high wall lining the straightaway, toward the garages at the end of the track.

My phone rang, and I turned away to answer it.

"Hey Meredith," Emily said. "The buses are here. The 4-H bus is headed for the track, and the high school bus to the house. Footmen are at the north wing to receive the theater kids at the auditorium, and Mable will help the art mentor set up in the gallery."

"Thanks for the update, Emily." I checked my watch. "We're on schedule to view the exhibit at three and showtime at four."

"Sounds great," she replied, hanging up.

The high-pitched growl of go-kart engines sounded across the track as the staff finished preparations. I made my way to the parking area at the near end of the bleachers. The bright-yellow bus lumbered into view, pulling off the paved road and up to the gate.

The din of excited children exploded as the rumble of the bus died. The doors swung open, and a man outfitted in shorts and a 4-H Club T-shirt descended the stairs, a whistle around his neck. "Hi Meredith, good to see you again."

"You too, Jeff," I replied, shaking his hand. "How's the 4-H Club treating you?"

"It's great," he said. "We've had some amazing after-school enrichment programs this year, and most of this bunch are either back from summer camp or will be leaving shortly. It's been a wonderful experience for so many of them, especially the rural kids. And as always, we can't thank the Collins family enough for all their contributions and support. The agriculture program William put together has given them some real hands-on experience learning about food and farming. Some of the kids are hoping to get a peek at his collection of tractors. Anyway, where should we put them?"

I glanced over my shoulder, spotting William on his way back with Jason. "Have them gather around the tables. William will greet them and send them down to the garages. Our mechanic, Eddie, is dealing with an issue at the house, but he has extra help on hand, so look for Travis. He'll help you out. And they can help themselves to the snacks as well."

"Great, thank you." He hopped up the steps and blew two sharp blasts on his whistle. "Alright, listen up! We're gathering at those tables over there." He pointed, "You see them? I want you on your best behavior out there, and no roughhousing. We've got toddlers running around, so be careful. Grab something at the tables if you want, but no messes. Use the trash cans and recycling bins. Understood?"

"Yes, Coach!" they shouted.

"Okay," Jeff said, taking up position just outside the door. "Let's move it, nice and easy. No shoving."

All around twelve years old, carrying backpacks or duffels, the kids filed past us. Laughing and yelling, they soon broke into a run toward the tables.

"No!" Jeff sighed in exasperation. He turned to me. "Did I say no running, Meredith?"

"You did not," I confirmed, laughing.

"No running!" he shouted in vain.

"I count twenty-seven," I said as the last of them jumped from the steps of the bus.

"Good, let's hope it stays that way."

As we trailed behind the kids to the tables, Jeff extended a hand as William approached.

"Hello, Coach," William greeted. "How's this year's crop of young leaders looking?"

"Couldn't ask for better, William. Good to see you."

"Excellent," William said. "Shall I say a few words before we set them loose?"

"Absolutely," Jeff agreed, giving a short burst on his whistle. "Listen up! Before we get started, please give Mr. Collins your undivided attention."

"Hello, children," William called. "How are you enjoying the summer racing program so far?" A cheer went up. "Wonderful! My family and I would like to welcome you to the fifth annual Collins Classic, a fun little race we like to put on for you 4-H kids."

"Why are you bringing these kids here?" someone asked.

William laughed, "I thought they would like something with a motor, but a little smaller than a tractor."

"Yes, we know how you love farming and animals," the same voice responded.

William continued, "Now, this is all about having fun today, but with trophies for first, second, and third place, perhaps you'll discover a love for competitive racing. If so, talk to Coach and we'll see about enrolling you in the Collins Racing Team, where you'll learn how to hone your racing skills and compete against the best racers in the region. But for now, just go out there and have fun. And be safe!"

Another cheer went up as the children danced and jumped about. Jeff held up a hand. "Okay, everyone.

Let's head over to the garages—no running—for the safety drill."

It was hard to tell who was more excited, the kids or William. He urged the children on, clapping and waving his hands as they went. Helen wrapped an arm around his waist. "You really love the 4-H program, don't you?"

"Of course, my dear. Another FFA," William said, watching the kids flood up the lane. "That's the future right there."

"The kids have a lot of fond memories of their karting years," Bill said, grabbing a granola bar off a table.

"This one's about ready to get started," Emma remarked, coddling her infant daughter as we laughed.

The small clay track was built to accommodate both Junior and Cadet classes for speedway racing—entailing four left turns and two straightaways. Nine Cadet karts sat before the starting line, their sleek fiberglass bodywork hugging the small chassis, each decorated with colorful graphics and decals. The race would have three heats of nine racers, and each heat would be allowed one practice run. The top three of each would then compete in the final heat. Eddie's flaggers were posted throughout the track, with an announcer in the box ready to give a play-by-play through the PA system.

The afternoon flew by as the Collins family and their friends cheered the kids on, and by two o'clock, two boys and a girl stood on the small plywood winner's podium before the bleachers. Trophies raised above their heads, their fellow racers applauded their victory, with only a few pouting faces in the bunch.

"Congratulations to our victors!" William shouted, addressing the crowd. "And for those not on the podium today—I repeat, *not* on the podium—remember this. You have won something today that the champions have not. Knowledge. I am often asked what I would change if I could go back, and the answer is nothing. Win or lose, all things in life help you build character. And when you have to pick yourself up off the ground, that's when you learn the most. It teaches you grit and determination, which will serve you far better in life than any trophy. So, pick yourselves up, for you are now better armed than you were yesterday—which means you'll approach your next challenge with hard-earned secrets that will help you succeed in the next endeavor and the one after that. In this way, my friends, there is no such thing as losing."

CHAPTER
3

With the races over, William gave several kids a quick tour of the barn, showing off his collection of vintage tractors. As the family piled into golf carts, Coach told us he'd walk the kids to the house to help them burn off some energy. As the cart bumped along the manicured landscape, I called Emily. "The family will be at the gallery in a bit. They're going to freshen up at the house first."

"Sounds great," she replied. "We're all set. The art mentor and his students are standing by, and the director is going through final lighting checks with her crew."

"Great, see you soon."

A short time later, the family began trickling into the north wing. Long corridors opened up into a series of open rooms with light-brown hardwood floors and white walls. With large windows for sunlight and high ceilings lined with track lighting at strategic points, the rooms housed simple leather benches of varying lengths before certain wall hangings, interspersed amongst occasional white pedestals showcasing statues and pottery. Throughout, artwork and photography of every style and size adorned the walls. High-schoolers and 4-H kids browsed the rooms in hushed tones, some of them outfitted in stage costumes—theater students waiting for showtime.

As we made our way through the gallery, William tapped a loafer on the hardwood floor. "I still don't see why we couldn't carpet the gallery. My entire home was carpeted as a boy. It's soothing to the sole."

Helen smirked. "Which soul, dear? The foot or the spirit?"

"Well, both I suppose." William said. "It's better for the joints as well."

"We'll consider it, darling," Helen assured him.

I raised an eyebrow at her.

She glanced at William, shaking her head at me when he wasn't looking.

I hid my smile behind a hand.

Along the way, William stopped at a few of his favorite pieces—mostly farm, landscape, and Western art by the likes of Russell Houston and Tim Cox. William's pride in his western art pieces reflected on his face.

The two northernmost rooms had been cleared for the student exhibit, and here the family gathered to peruse their latest creations. The director of the Collins Arts Mentorship Program, Andres Trevino, walked alongside William, Helen, and me, answering questions and introducing students.

"Look at this piece, darling," William remarked, studying a large oil-on-canvas landscape depicting the oak-studded foothills of Northern California.

"Lovely," she replied. "It looks like Napa Valley, doesn't it?"

A boy of about sixteen fidgeted nearby. "This is Cameron," Andres said. "He's one of our finest young artists when it comes to landscapes."

"Well done, young man," Helen said.

"Thank you," Cameron mumbled with a shy smile.

"Tell us about it," said William. "It's remarkable."

Cameron huffed a nervous laugh. "Thank you. I took a trip with my family a few years ago to Lake Tahoe, and we stopped at a restaurant on the way. This was the view from our table. As near as I can remember, anyway."

"From memory," Helen said, impressed. "Very remarkable indeed. Will you be going on to study art?"

"I'd like to," Cameron replied. "I'm looking into schools now. Hopefully, I'll be accepted."

"You've nothing to fear in that regard, I'm sure," William said. He dropped his voice to a whisper. "And we have something in mind to help you afford it." He put a finger to his lips. "Keep that under your hat for now, my boy."

Cameron beamed; his eyes wide as he nodded his head. "Okay!"

***

A short time later, the lights dimmed in the gallery, calling us to the small auditorium at the end of the wing. With seating for about fifty, the architects had scratched their heads at the request it be added to the blueprints when the estate was being built. Yet it had seen a good amount of use over the years—both for fun, family events and many school plays, from grade school to high school, and even some private shows from local theater companies. Standing room only, the extended Collins family, art students, and 4-H kids filled the seats, with most of the staff lining the walls, taking a break from their duties to catch the show.

The play was called *The Birthday Cake*, a one-act comedy written and performed by aspiring playwrights and actors from the local high school's drama department, all of whom were a part of the Collins Arts Mentorship Program. Based on the Collins family, it followed a crazed chef named Cilliam Wollins on his quest to create the perfect cake for the patriarch's seventy-fifth birthday. With over a dozen cakes failing to pass Cilliam's muster, the kitchen soon found itself without ingredients. He sent the staff to search far and wide, but the nearby towns and villages were mysteriously barren of supplies. Mimicking William's reputation for dedication and refusing to lose, the chef began improvising, using whatever he could find to test strange new recipes.

"Let it not be said that I, Cilliam Wollins, balked in the face of a challenge!" the chef cried, tossing sneakers, a houseplant, and other random items into a large bowl of water. "I shall create a new recipe, the likes of which have never been seen in this kingdom or any other. It will be the envy of all, including that charlatan, Chef Shifty from the neighboring kingdom!"

Stirring and splashing as he continued to rant, his sous chef burst onto the stage. "Chef! I found some old ingredients in the back of the walk-in!"

"Excellent!" Cillian shouted. "What are they?"

"Uh, let's see," replied the sous chef, glancing off-stage. "I found some snakes, snails, and puppy dog tails."

"Imbecile!" cried the chef. "Those ingredients are for something else entirely!"

The audience broke into laughter. Turning in my seat, I raised a questioning eyebrow at Chef Eliot, where he stood near the exit. He nodded, giving me a thumbs-up, confirming the accuracy of the recipe.

As the play continued, it was discovered that Chef Shifty was responsible for the disappeared foodstuffs— he had purchased every ingredient in the kingdom, in an attempt to sabotage the king's big day. But in his experiments, Cilliam discovered a new type of frosting that changed hue depending on the angle from which it was viewed, giving off bright, vibrant colors like a kaleidoscope. Yet with his other experiments resulting in disaster, he still lacked a proper cake. Cilliam called an emergency meeting of the local Cooking Guild, demanding that Chef Shifty make his stash of ingredients available for purchase.

Using a meat tenderizer as a gavel, the Head Chef called the meeting to order. "Chef Shifty, you stand accused of purloining precious provisions in pursuit of petulant purposes. How do you plead?"

"Not guilty, Chef," Shifty said, twirling a large, oily mustache. "I purchased those items from your kingdom legally, in preparation for my queen's ninetieth birthday. I've done nothing wrong."

"Objection!" cried Cilliam. "If he's innocent, why is he twirling his mustache like that? Only villains do that. Besides, it goes against regulations. Where is your hairnet, sir?"

"Sustained," the Head Chef called. "Chef Bollins is right. You're acting super evil right now. And you should know better than to appear in session without a hairnet."

"Apologies, Chef," Shifty conceded, still twirling. "The truth is, the queen doesn't see so well anymore, and I need to make the cake as big as possible. The biggest cake in the world!"

"If that is true," Cilliam interrupted, "then why are you still twirling your moustache?"

"It's a compulsion, okay?" Shifty defended. "I can't help it."

"Fine," Cilliam said. "I have an idea. Let's make a deal."

The audience broke into applause as the lights faded for the final scene change, soon revealing the whole cast gathered around the king and the queen from the neighboring kingdom.

Chef Bollins stood, addressing the audience as if it were the royal court. "Lords and Ladies, nobles of the court, I am honored to help bring our two kingdoms together on this auspicious occasion to celebrate the tandem birthdays of the beloved king and queen. In a first for our great nations, we found ourselves confronted with a tremendous opportunity, and I am pleased to report that we did not shy from it." He pointed off-stage. "May this first-of-its-kind birthday cake serve as a symbol for the long and prosperous future of our two houses!"

A large prop was wheeled out, to the applause of the court—a tall, multi-tiered cake of papier-mâché. Small strobe lights shone from the many small holes in each tier, bathing the auditorium in dancing, multicolored light. The Collins family crest appeared on the largest tier, next to another crest representing the queen.

"Begging the court's pardon," Chef Bollins said, "but you'll have to use your hands. I used all the forks in my experiments."

The lights faded and the curtain fell, eliciting cheers and applause from the audience. As the curtain opened, the lights came up to reveal a standing ovation. The cast took turns stepping downstage to take a bow, and various members of the Collins family were there to greet them with bouquets of flowers. After many hugs and much milling about, the director brought William up on stage. The cast moved left and right, giving him the spotlight as the crowd quieted down.

"Well done, one and all," William enthused, causing another round of cheers and applause. "I haven't laughed like that in a long while. That Chef Bollins, he's a man after my own heart." The audience broke into laughter, the lead actor bowing to William from his spot near the wings. "And he had the right of it. I'm glad to see you take a few of my pearls of wisdom to heart. Competition, be it in business, sport, or just for fun, is an important aspect of life. But far more often than many think, cooperation serves far better than competition ever could. It's a fine lesson to carry with you."

William paused before continuing. "As is the lesson of never giving up. Did Chef Bollins even consider it? No, he improvised, adapted to the situation. Did he have any hope of finding a solution? He didn't care! He needed one, so he resolved to find it. And when convention failed him, as it sometimes will, he still remained unbothered. If you can't find a solution, *create* one. How, you ask, when the normal run of things no longer applies, when you have no choice but to throw out the book and come up with your own rules? By engaging those around you. Your best resources aren't tools or ingredients, it's collaboration. Two minds can succeed where one mind fails."

He smiled at the nodding heads in the audience. "I am often asked what my best talent is, and I think I have a bit of talent recognizing other talent. And I see a great deal of talent in this room. To ensure that it's given every opportunity to flourish, we have some wonderful news for you. All of those who complete at least two summer sessions of the Collins Arts Mentorship Program will be awarded a one-year scholarship to the arts college of their choice." He paused, scanning the eager faces. "But of course, only if they also teach Western art."

Andres wasn't joking about needing earplugs. The auditorium nearly shook with the thunderous cheers from the kids. Jumping around and hugging each other, with some shedding tears, it was an incredible moment. It took the director a full minute to regain control.

"And if there are any seniors in the first year of the program," William said, "worry not. You're eligible as well." A few of the seniors almost collapsed in relief, hugging their classmates as William continued. "Now, I do have another bit of news, but after that first bit, you probably aren't interested."

He studied his fingernails, dismissive of their prodding calls. "Oh, you do want to know? You're sure?" The children yelled and cheered and clapped, growing rowdier by the moment. "Well, okay, if you insist."

I could have heard a pin drop.

"This is a spur-of-the-moment decision, so we don't

have any details yet, but we'll also be sending you on field trips to surrounding campuses, giving you a sense of what you have to look forward to while helping you decide where to pursue your college careers."

Where the kids got the energy to be so loud, so often, I didn't know, but they sent their voices to the rafters once more, rushing to William on the stage and burying him in hugs. He found Helen in the audience, reaching out to her and shouting for help as they jostled him about. The director waded in like a ref in a dog pile, half-amused, half-concerned, calling for calm and quiet. Eventually, the kids settled, giving William some breathing room. And as usual, I couldn't tell who was happier—him or the children.

CHAPTER
4

By seven o'clock, an energetic waltz from the string quartet echoed off the high ceiling of the ballroom, the notes dancing with the large crystal chandelier at its center before floating down among the many guests, infusing all it touched with a celebratory air. The tall windows looked out on the eastern portion of the lake; their mahogany shutters partially closed against the low sun. To the right of the quartet, a long table at the edge of the dance floor sat laden with all manner of wrapped presents and decorative envelopes. Several couples made use of the dance floor, while William's partners at the firm talked shop at the surrounding tables. Childhood friends from the country milled about in small groups, talking and laughing about old times.

I watched as William, his back pressed against the wall, surveyed the crowd. His face a masked smile, but knowing him so well, I knew he was torn between his finely tuned sense of public persona and his personal desire to run to the garage where he found solitude in the aloneness. What most people did not understand was that William was two different people and given his preference, he would rather be tinkering on a tractor or rocking on the front porch gazing out at the magnificent views. He only made a minor fuss about having to dress fancy for this event. I marveled at his chameleon ability to manage both with such grace and dignity.

Turning my attention back to the room, I was enchanted by the ladies in evening gowns of the latest cuts and richest colors. They stood out like gemstones in a sea of straight-backed men in dark tuxedos. All came and went as they pleased, taking in the air on the veranda or mingling in adjacent drawing rooms for quieter conversation. Servers made the rounds, their trays laden with selections of nonalcoholic spirits and ciders, as well as delicious hors d'oeuvres.

My dressmaker had outdone herself. The dark-teal, high-neck chiffon with an open back and ruched waistband fit me like a glove, and for once, the matching heels were actually comfortable—it was a shame they were hidden by the floor-length hem. In lieu of a clutch, I had her sew a secret pocket near the hip, hidden by the subtle vertical folds where the gown met the waistline. With my phone on vibrate, I could be kept apprised of the logistics of the evening, as well as the simmering peach tree virus situation. Though my dressmaker had been scandalized by the unusual request, for me it was a matter of principle—I'll not be without pockets, no matter the occasion.

A sparkling soda in hand, I surveyed the festivities from the sidelines, soon flagged over by a small group near some tables. An older man in a midnight-blue waistcoat held out a hand as I approached. "Meredith, how wonderful to see you."

"And you, Antonio, so glad you could make it." He turned to his two companions. "You've met my wife, Kelly."

"Of course, lovely to see you again, Kelly."

"You as well, Meredith."

"And this," Antonio continued, "is Anita Luna, of Chez Luna fame. She was just telling us of her rise to greatness."

"Of course," I replied, shaking her hand, "your restaurants are all the rage. It's a pleasure to meet you."

"Likewise, thank you," Anita tipped her head.

"I recall him going on at length about you during his trips to Southern California years ago," I said. "Is that where you met?"

Anita smiled. "Yes, about eight years ago. I was the executive chef of a little-known boutique restaurant in Malibu, where I was experimenting with various fusion dishes. Mostly Mexican and various Asian cuisine. One busy Friday night, a server told me a patron wanted to speak with me. It was William. He asked me all kinds of questions, trying to get a sense of what I was trying to accomplish. He was incredibly complimentary and encouraging. Looking back, I needed to hear those words far more than I realized. The culinary arts can be pretty cutthroat."

I nodded. "I can appreciate that. Law can be the same."

"Over the next year or so, he'd stop in for dinner at least once a month while staying at his vacation home—sometimes he'd bring his wife, sometimes with business associates, always asking questions and offering encouragement. Eventually, he asked me if I'd be interested in assembling a private four-course tasting meal for him and two friends. I obliged, discovering that night his friends were among the top food critics in the country."

"Goodness," I breathed, "that must have been nerve racking."

Anita laughed. "It was, and I was grateful William hadn't warned me ahead of time. But I was so nervous, I had my head server deliver each course. I forbade him from giving me any indication of their reaction, though I couldn't help but notice that most of the dishes came back barely touched. I was rapidly losing hope, but I pushed on through to the dessert. I made it special. I made a puff pastry like a cream puff. Mr. Collins always insisted because his mother used to make it on special occasions. And he reminded me to always try to use peaches in the dessert."

The group laughed at the reminder of William's passion for peaches.

"Then it was time for the moment of truth—William summoned me to the table. I was prepared to be torn to ribbons, but the critics were surprisingly receptive. As I answered their questions, however, my heart continued to drop. They weren't particularly impressed. But they did express a bit of intrigue."

She laughed, her eyes drifting to the ceiling as though reliving the moment. "Honestly, they were so hard to read, I wasn't sure what to make of the discussion. But William cleared it up in short order. He told me that he and his friends wanted to send me on an open-ended training trip. I was to study with some of the top chefs at the most experimental restaurants throughout the United States. Of course, I was speechless. Before I could stop myself, I blurted out, 'Why?' I'll never forget what William said. 'Anita, I'm not interested in perfection. I'm interested in potential. And while your ideas are a bit raw, I see a tremendous hidden potential in you. So well hidden, in fact, that you don't even see it yourself. My colleagues have confirmed what I've suspected all along—your dishes, your concepts, show the makings of a wholly unique take on fusion cuisine, and it's one worth supporting. Soon enough, you'll come to see your potential for yourself. Then, there will be no stopping you.'"

Antonio glanced at Kelly, then me. "That's our William."

"From there," Anita continued, "I spent the next two years traveling, working with some amazing mentors, learning more about my craft than I ever thought possible. And William was there checking in every step of the way, always offering encouragement and a word of advice. As I defined and developed my own style—expressing all that hidden potential William kept going on about—he and I began discussing how to bring it to the world. With a great deal of hard work and his unwavering support, I now have a Michelin three-star restaurant in Malibu, another in London, and the Chez Luna chain of restaurants throughout California, providing a contemporary take on French-infused Mexican cuisine. I'm also looking into a franchise of food trucks that employ specific cooking techniques to provide a fast-delivery approach to our signature fusion dishes."

Kelly nodded to her husband. "As two loyal fans of your work who have been to both of your Michelin-rated restaurants on several occasions, it couldn't have happened to a more talented chef."

"Thank you very much," Anita replied, giving a slight bow. "Now, if you'll excuse me, Chef Elliot has invited me into his kitchen to talk shop about tonight's hors d'oeuvres. It was a pleasure meeting you all."

"Thank you, Anita," I said. "Be sure to tell chef they're proving to be a big hit."

"Remarkable," Antonio said as Anita disappeared into the crowd. "How is William able to see things in his family and others that no one else can—including the people themselves?"

"The more time you spend mingling tonight, the more you'll find that the vast majority of those gathered share a similar story," I told the couple. "Nearly everyone here owes a debt of gratitude to William, me included." My phone buzzed in my pocket. Two short bursts—a text from Emily.

"I'd better check in with things. Enjoy your evening, you two."

"Thank you, Meredith," Kelly replied.

Ducking into the hallway, I found a quiet corner and checked my phone. *Ralph fixed the walk-in. It's holding steady at 38 degrees. Should the racks be brought back up?* I called her.

She picked up on the first ring. "Hi, Meredith."

I could hear the bustling sounds of the kitchen in the background. "Hey, Emily. That's great to hear about the walk-in. It's entirely up to chef about the racks. Whatever's best for him."

"Okay, I'll tell him. One of the guest's cars broke down on the way to the north lawn."

"Is Eddie handling it?"

"Yeah, he's bringing it back to the garage with the tow truck. He said it looks like it just overheated, but he needs to check a few things to be sure. There's a small chance it's something more serious. Whatever it is, he should have it up and running before departure, assuming the guest is staying for the fireworks."

I smiled at a passing couple on their way to the ballroom. "Whose car is it?"

"Dennis Abrams. Do you know him?"

"Yes, he's worked with Helen on a number of projects. Locate her for me quick, would you?"

"Sure, no problem." Emily paused.

I knew she turned to her walkie-talkie when I heard. "All servers, who has eyes on Helen?" Another pause. "Thank you." Her voice returned to my ear. "Meredith, she's in the west drawing room with William, greeting the next flight arrival."

"Great, thank you. I'll keep an eye out for Dennis and see if she knows his whereabouts. If Eddie needs parts to repair the car, tell him to take from William's collection if he finds something compatible. If not, tell him to call Sanford's, in town. We do a lot of business with them. They work late so he should be able to get them on the phone. They'll likely have whatever we need on hand. Tell Eddie we'll pay extra for immediate delivery."

"Will do."

"Anything else?" I heard what sounded like a stack of plates crash to the floor.

"Nope, all under control here!"

I laughed. "Keep texting with any issues. I'll answer as soon as I can. And call for any emergencies."

"Will do, thanks Meredith."

I made my way to the west drawing room, taking the scenic route to the east entrance first to assure all was in order. The dark hardwood floors and molding contrasted the rich colors of the tapestries and area rugs leading to the main double staircase, its wide steps and hand-carved banisters descending to a large, vaulted foyer. Moving through a maze of hallways, past the library, main kitchen and a series of studies and sitting rooms, I came to a large drawing room adorned with antique furniture, more western art wall hangings, and an ornate fireplace with low flames.

Guests arriving by helicopter—mostly old friends of William's who lived out in the country—were brought through the southwest entrance to a large half-bath, allowing them to freshen up from their trip before being received. William and Helen stood near the fire, waiting for the arrivals to show.

William was looking himself over in a nearby mirror, tugging at his collar and fiddling with his bowtie. It was another reminder to me of the dichotomy that the man who was more comfortable in holey jeans was the same man here tonight in his custom-tailored tuxedo.

He face broke into a broad grin when he saw me approaching. "There's our master of ceremonies! You look astonishing, my dear."

"Why, thank you, Mr. Collins," I replied. "You clean up pretty well yourself."

"Bah," he scoffed, attempting to straighten his tie. "I don't see why blue jeans and a polo shirt couldn't suffice."

Helen took his tie in her hands, weaving the ends around with a practiced hand. "Special occasions call for special attire, darling. You'll be back in blue jeans in a few hours."

William harrumphed again. "I suppose."

Helen wore a floor-length gown of deep blue and flowing waves, accentuated by a sparkling sapphire necklace and earrings, her silver hair radiant in a classic low chignon that showed off the matching shawl draped across her shoulders.

I shook my head. "Helen, you've outdone yourself. How do you do it?"

"Thank you, my dear, as have you. I find that the secret lies in the pockets." She slid a few folds to the side at her hip, revealing a hidden pocket.

I laughed, revealing my own. "They certainly make the gown, don't they?"

William shook his head. "I'm all for secret pockets, but if you aren't using them to house snacks, I don't know why you bother."

Helen tsked. "I have a difficult enough time keeping your hands off me as it is. If I carried snacks on me, you'd never give me a moment's peace."

William lifted his chin, peering at Helen with mock sternness. "I concede your point, my dear. That's fair enough." We broke into laughter.

"Helen, have you seen Dennis Abrams?" I asked. "There's a bit of trouble with his car. It's being taken care of, but I wanted to see how long he planned on staying."

"I saw him on the veranda nearest the water about half an hour ago," she replied. "He's a quiet sort, preferring open air and calmer surroundings. You'll likely still find him there."

"Wonderful, thank you," I said. "I'll check there. If either of you need me, just ask any server with a headset. They can get a message to me right away."

"Thank you, Meredith," William said, "but do try to have some fun tonight."

"I always have fun," I winked, "provided I'm not sent on any wild goose chases looking for old fools."

"Well, this old fool would very much like to know more about his secret birthday present. Surely, you can give me a hint by now?"

"I'm afraid not," I answered. "There are still too many things in motion. You'll have to be patient."

"Patience is my specialty," William stated, bouncing on the balls of his feet in frustration. He leveled an accusing gaze at Helen.

"I'm sure I know nothing about it," she said, inspecting her shawl.

"So, it's conspiracy then, is it?"

I shared a knowing look with Helen as I headed for the hallway. "Patience, William," I called over my shoulder.

Dennis was indeed staying for the fireworks, and with that issue under control, my phone buzzed again. A continuous vibration, denoting a call. It was Dana, the Collins' corporate attorney. I'd been hoping to hear from her.

"Hey Dana, what's the word?"

"Hi, Meredith. I've secured the purchase of two small stone fruit orchards in Placer and Butte Counties, as well as a larger one in Yolo County. All three are confirmed for the new strain of virus, according to Victor's field agents at FRD. I also just got off the phone with Victor. He's in talks with representatives at the California Department of Food and Agriculture and a few other organizations. Some are still of the mind that this is an established strain, despite the fact that they haven't been able to curb the spread through traditional mitigation protocols. He's trying to press home the fact that tests are showing something else altogether—attempting to raise the alarm without raising alarm, you know?"

"Yes, it's going to take some time to get the results in the right hands and raise awareness. I'm not sure how many orchards William will want, so keep working on that list of potential acquisitions. The three you've secured should be enough to get us started. Victor has people tracking the spread on his end, with a running list of who owns what, so we'll be able to give William all the data he needs to decide who to acquire and who to collaborate with."

"Sounds good. I'll update you tomorrow."

"That's okay. It's what William wants. It reminds him of his childhood. Besides, it's a land investment first, business second. And I'm out looking at peach farms to buy now. It's not a moneymaker, but we are buying land that'll increase in value."

Heading up the steps, back to the ballroom, I debated calling Victor. I hoped he'd be arriving soon.

CHAPTER
5

Putting the issue out of my mind as best I could, I made the rounds with the guests. The ballroom was near capacity now, with the majority of the dance floor and nearly every table occupied, along with standing groups of various size milling about.

At a small group of half a dozen or so guests, I recognized Nigel Barker, the CEO of New Day PR, our public relations firm. He nodded me over as he turned his attention back to the man at the center of the discussion.

"Good to see you, Meredith," Nigel said, keeping his voice low. "Do you know Allen Simmons, the host of the Jurispodence podcast?"

"You too, Nigel. No, never met him, but I know William is a fan." I extended my hand to Allen. He was a stocky man somewhere in his thirties, with an exciting air about him.

He grasped my hand in greeting, then returned seamlessly to the conversation, eliciting a round of laughter. "It's like I said," he picked up where he left off. "Back then, the podcasting industry was like the wild west. It just refused to map onto any established industry like TV, film, or publishing, let alone radio. My two friends and I were still finishing up our law degrees and just making it up as we went along, not really concerned about growth or ad revenue or turning our work into a long-term thing. But even after UCLA, as we started establishing our careers, we kept the podcast going, more as a fun little side project than anything else. We pretty much agreed on the direction we should take it, focusing on the news angle and deep-dive discussions into the latest decisions at the federal and state levels, along with broad takes on the nature of law and the court of public opinion."

He took a sip of what looked like ginger ale. "As the years passed and we continued to grow—mostly through networking than any solid marketing strategy or organized social media campaigns—we started to take it more seriously. Each of us was doing well at our respective firms, but we kept harboring this love for the podcast. The only problem was that we were becoming jaded. Now out of college about five or six years, our experience had washed away our youthful optimism. The legal world was dog-eat-dog, which wasn't necessarily a bad thing, but none of us had really landed at the right firm. Nothing felt like home. I think that's why we continued the podcast through those years—despite how little money we made with it—it was the closest we had come to something we enjoyed doing. Despite our success moving up the ladder in our careers, it was all just more clients and court dates and hearings and—"

Allen closed his eyes and started snoring, resulting in a ripple of laughter through the gathering.

"Don't get me wrong, we still loved the law. It was still the exciting, ever-changing, always-fascinating subject that had piqued our interest in college—we just hadn't found where we fit in yet. And as for the podcast, the more we looked around, the more we saw the same type of content we were creating. The medium had gotten very crowded, very quickly. No matter what we covered, there were a dozen other shows covering the same thing, using the same format. And worse, some had devolved into a hyperfocus on the celebrity crowd, raking in all kinds of ad revenue by spouting the most useless content that did nothing to inform the audience. I mean, we're all for entertainment, but there's got to be some substance in there as well."

A man I didn't recognize raised a hand. "I may or may not have been a strong supporter of those shows, back when I didn't know any better."

Allen's eyes went wide, pointing his finger at the man. "You see? It's his fault!" We laughed as the man hung his head in mock shame. "So, there we were, several years into our careers, generally unhappy with our professional lives, not really sure what to do about our podcast. We decided to spend the next several months on a fact-finding mission. We listened to every law podcast episode we could lay our ears on, dissecting what they did and how they did it, what we agreed with and what we didn't, all in an effort to find our own path—something no one else was doing, that still filled a void and provided value, and above all, something we could have fun doing. And that's how we came across the idea for Jurispodence—a funny, slightly irreverent take on the law news of the day, with a primary focus on making the law fun and fascinating, and a secondary focus on information and expert insight. What we wanted was something like those satire news shows, but in the law podcasting niche."

I was fascinated by the discussion unfolding. "What obstacles did you encounter?"

"The real challenge was committing to this new format. We were bursting at the seams with ideas, but we had no way of knowing if it would be successful. Keep in mind that even today, finding solid metrics on podcasts is nearly impossible. Sure, certain platforms share total downloads or subscriber numbers, but there are so many podcast hosting platforms, all with missing—or at best, disagreeing—metrics, that it makes gauging any particular show's popularity incredibly difficult. You have to suss out a variety of less-than-concrete data—gauging word-of-mouth from podcast forums and communities, evaluating the degree to which platforms push particular shows, and worst of all, simply taking the word of any platform that bothered to release some semblance of information. While the top handful of successful pods in any given genre is pretty obvious, for every one of them, there are a thousand others doing the same or similar type of content—so what set them apart? And above all, was it worth basing the future of our podcast on such shaky information?"

Allen flagged down a passing server and grabbed a glass from the tray. "Hey, would it be possible to get my friends here some coffee? I think I'm losing them." Another ripple of laughter as the smiling server melted into the crowd. "All of this is to say that we had a vision, but we had no idea if it would work. We went for it anyway, and the first few years of our new format were rough. We lost half our audience almost immediately, which was a huge blow. What little ad revenue we were making disappeared. And booking interviews wasn't easy. Guests wanted to discuss the nitty-gritty, sharing their super-serious takes on various hot-button issues. But eventually, we got back up to two episodes per week and found a little rhythm. Listenership was stable, with a few minor upticks, and we figured we would likely be making some ad revenue again inside six months." He held up a finger, looking each of us in the eyes as he spoke. "But most importantly, we were *having fun*. We loved what we were doing. The nine-to-five grind was worth it, just to spend our nights and weekends doing something we enjoyed. However, our main issue was the same it had always been—episode frequency. One thing that had always held us back was that the biggest pods released a new episode daily. We just couldn't produce at that pace, not with jobs and family obligations. As those first years of the new format went by, we began to accept that the pod was never going to be anything but a passion project. And that's when I met William.

"Little did we know he was a podcast fan, always listening while flying around the world in his private jet, similar to the one I'm totally going to buy someday. How our little show came up on his phone, I'll never know. But on some random Tuesday, I get a call from him, and he wants to meet in Los Angeles to talk. He said a law podcast had never made him laugh like ours had, and after listening to several more episodes, he wanted to learn a bit more about us. I'm always up for new opportunities, and of course I'd heard about William—the man's on the cover of a different magazine every month. That meeting, ladies and gentlemen, changed our lives forever."

I spotted the waiter waving for my attention. He tipped his fingers to his lips seeking confirmation about serving coffee. I discretely shook my head 'no' and he smiled before disappearing again.

"We had a long talk, which was the first of many things that surprised me about him—I was expecting at most an hour-long lunch, but we spent the entire afternoon together. I told him much the same I've told you here tonight, except for one important distinction—in a decidedly unbusinesslike move, I found myself trying to talk him out of the possibilities. It wasn't a question of finding the right guests or even the impossible challenge of releasing daily episodes, it was my lack of faith in the content itself. We'd received plenty of criticism over the years of our format's lack of depth, some finding it nothing more than fluff that pretended to be substantive. I didn't think it could become a leader in the space even with the help of someone like William. It wasn't what people wanted."

Nigel asked, "What happened then?"

"And that's when he dropped some bombshell knowledge on me—sometimes, on very rare occasions, audiences are presented with something they didn't even know they wanted. And it was our vision of the show that had created that space." Allen puffed up his chest and lifted his chin. "'Living inside your vision, Allen.'" The gathering burst into laughter. His impersonation of William was uncanny. "'Living inside your vision is the key to making it a reality.' And he was right. He pointed out how my partners and I had spent the past few years living inside the kind of show *we* wanted to listen to. And our vision was all the stronger and more valid because we kept it through the worst of times. My lack of faith in the show was a smokescreen, its only purpose to hide the truth—my actions had already shown an unshakable faith in what we were doing, despite my feelings to the contrary."

I lifted my glass in a toast and everyone in the group followed my lead. "Here's to your perseverance and William's wisdom!"

Allen beamed. "Can you believe it? One of the most successful personal injury attorneys in the country, owner of the most famous firm in California, a man with huge investments in half a dozen industries, convincing *me* to take a chance on myself. And as I'm sure you're all aware, there's no saying 'no' to William. So, my partners and I dove in with both feet. Funded and advised by none other than William Collins himself, including some incredibly innovative marketing strategies he schooled us on, we were given carte blanche to create a law podcast unlike any other. And today, we're a household name, with a waiting list of other household names clamoring for a guest spot."

A round of cheers and applause went up from the small group. Allen raised his hands, shaking his head. "Believe me, I'm as surprised as you are."

My phone buzzed another text. I pulled away, nodding a goodbye to Nigel as Allen answered another question from the group.

It was Emily. *Clouding up despite earlier forecast. Local radar shows possible showers.* I gave her a call.

"Hey Meredith. Jerry, the lead pyrotechnician, says the fireworks can continue as long as the rain isn't too bad. If it's just a light shower, we should be fine. But it's definitely a wait-and-see kind of thing. My concern is the tables on the veranda. There's over four dozen of them."

"All without umbrellas. Shoot, we didn't plan for this."

"It's my fault," Emily said, "I should have thought of it."

"Nonsense, you're doing great," I assured her. "What do we say about blame?"

"It's for those without solutions."

"That's right. What are our options? Did you try the equipment rental service?"

"Yes, they closed at seven."

"It's okay, I've got the owner's number. While I sort that out, tell Thomas to have his footmen take every available clothing rack from the laundry and use them to move all guest coats and accessories to the south drawing room. Make sure the tickets stay intact. I'll call you back in a minute."

I found the owner's number and called him. "Hi Jake, it's Meredith at the Collins estate. There's a bit of an issue. Have you seen the weather?"

"Umbrellas!" the man thundered in my ear. "The weather's been clear for weeks and it wasn't supposed to rain today. I'm so sorry, Meredith. How can I help?"

"No worries, Jake. I'm hoping you can gather a quick team to load a truck and get here as soon as possible. It's about a forty-five-minute trip if they don't speed. We'll cover overtime, and they'll walk away with a generous tip and some pretty amazing hors d'oeuvres. How's that sound?"

"You had me at hors d'oeuvres. I'll be there myself. I'm calling my crew now."

"Thanks so much, Jake, I appreciate it. A valet will hop in with you at the gate and direct you to the west entrance."

On my way to the south drawing room, I called Emily back. "The umbrellas will be here by nine. Alert Marcus at the east gate to wave them through and to let you know when they arrive. Have Thomas post a valet at the gate to bring the truck to the west entrance. When Marcus gives the word, send all available staff to the west entrance—coordinate with Thomas, Mable, and chef to see how many they can spare. The umbrellas slide into heavy ornate bases that go beneath the tables, so break the staff into teams of two. Get as many teams as you can, but don't spread the servers too thin. Use your best judgment. And have a footman sent to the south drawing room with a velvet rope and two stands. We'll block off the room once I've cleared out any guests. I think that's everything. Call or text if you need me."

"Understood," Emily replied, hanging up.

My phone buzzed again. A text from Victor, stopping me in my tracks.

My team just confirmed the virus in South Carolina.

CHAPTER
6

At the top of the staircase leading to the south drawing room, I called Victor.

"Hi, Meredith. I've got you on speaker. I'm about half an hour out. Sorry I'm running late."

"No problem, Victor. Well, this isn't great news. Your team is sure?"

"Yes, the results just came back from a lab outside Charlotte, just over the border, showing the same markers as those found in California—highly resistant and faster growing. My people have gathered samples from two major orchards across two northern counties so far, and the story is the same wherever they go. The farms discovered outbreaks last year and implemented mitigation techniques—isolating and destroying infected trees, sterilizing equipment, ramping up pest control, the usual. Certain crops took a minor hit in production last season, but no one thought anything of it. Just the cost of doing business. As the current season progressed, they found little to no reduction in the virus' presence—indicating high resistance—and worse, it may be spreading faster than last year. Harvests at these orchards are taking a bigger hit this year, causing concern at affected farms, but the industry as a whole is still sleeping on the issue, especially the small farmers.

"It's imperative we gather as much data as we can industry wide. California and South Carolina are two of the top producers in the country with Georgia right up there, too. We need to focus on at least the top three states and find out exactly where this strain is and how fast it's spreading. Anecdotal evidence shows there may be an exponential growth at play, here. If that's the case, entire crops will likely be devastated next year."

"We need more people," I mused.

"Absolutely. We need CROs."

"What are they?"

"Contract Research Organizations," Victor replied. "If this were a localized issue spanning a few counties in California, my firm would be able to handle it. But we're way beyond that, now. CROs specialize in life sciences, and I'm hoping they can assist with field work, at least in the beginning. We need to form a board that can coordinate with CROs, government agencies, universities, agricultural companies and individually owned farms— across multiple states. It's going to take a concerted effort to track, study, and develop new mitigation techniques. To be honest, I was kind of dreading this news. Catching something like this early, when it's localized, is one thing. The mosaic virus is quite varied, affecting many different fruits and vegetables to one degree or another. For peaches, it's generally rare and easy to control. But there's no way to know when you're dealing with a far more dangerous strain until it's too late. And now that it's an interstate issue, we're in entirely new depths."

I sighed. "At least the timing is good. We're sharing the news with William tonight, and I have no doubt he's really going to sink his teeth into this one. He'll light a fire under every agency and organization involved. There's also the fact that it's August. Most harvests are over, with the rest wrapping up over the next few weeks. There may be time to save next year's crop."

"It's possible, but there are a lot of factors at play, and we need a lot more information. There's still too much we don't know. Getting an accurate assessment of the problem is our top priority, and it could take months. Cooperation is going to be key."

"Which other states do you want to focus on?"

"California is by far the biggest producer in the country, with South Carolina a distant second. Georgia and Pennsylvania should be added to the list, and maybe New Jersey as well. Getting a sense of where it's showing up is important, but when it comes to next year's harvest, California and South Carolina are going to be the main priorities."

"Okay. It's probably best to assume the virus is going to show up everywhere. I'll talk to Dana and have her team start compiling data on South Carolina, Georgia, Pennsylvania, and New Jersey. We'll have a database of every farm, agency, university, and organization for each state."

"Sounds good," Victor said. "I have a few suggestions for CROs as well. I'll see you soon."

Hanging up with Victor, I called Dana as I continued on to the south drawing room. "Hi, Dana. Working late?"

"Always," Dana replied with a laugh. "What's up?"

"We need to expand our search. The virus has been confirmed in South Carolina."

"Uh-oh."

"Yeah, it's not ideal. I'm hoping you can expand your data-collection team for a few days. We need names, numbers, and emails for South Carolina, as well as Georgia, Pennsylvania, and New Jersey. Not just potential acquisitions, but every entity tied to the peach industry. The same goes for California. Do you know anything about CROs?"

"Sure do," Dana said. "We do some contract law in the pharmaceutical industry. I've got a pretty good database of them. I'll add them to the list."

"Wonderful, thank you. The sooner the better. You know William."

Dana laughed. "I do indeed. I'll be in touch by tomorrow afternoon with what we have so far."

"Great, speak to you then."

✳✳✳

The south drawing room held a few small groups, a popular stopover between the ballroom and the veranda.

I texted Emily. *Send 2 servers with hors d'oeuvres and 2 more with beverages to south drawing room. Have them wait for my signal.*

Half a dozen people surrounded a man I recognized, Don Peterson, one of William's oldest friends. The subtle crimson of his pocket square highlighted his thinning red hair as he regaled listeners with a story of when they first met.

"Sacramento Racing had seen a good amount of success in the nearly twenty years since I'd founded it, but by the mid-nineties, we were in steady decline. Looking back, I can point to a dozen reasons why, all culminating over several years, but by '96, all I felt was frustration and confusion. I had no idea how things had gotten so bad."

The group surrounding him were nodding their heads in unison.

"After all, I'd grown up around racing. My father got his start with stock cars in the sixties, and by the seventies, I was helping him tinker with the latest Indy car engines. We spent our weekends at the Riverside International Raceway, the Ontario Motor Speedway, and a dozen others throughout California and the South. It was such an exciting time for racing, back then."

Don sighed, coming back to the present. "Anyway, in 1980, I founded Sacramento Racing, where we designed and built the latest racing car engines. We had our own racing team, and over the years, we partnered with some big names in the automotive industry, even expanding into racing supply. We won a steady string of championships throughout numerous circle track racing series and race car circuits all over the world, really making a name for ourselves as innovators in engine design and regular podium-finishers."

"That must have been so exciting," one woman said.

Don nodded and stroked his chin. "But racing is a performance business, and somewhere along the way, we started to lose our touch. More accurately, I suppose, I started to lose my touch. Competition was as fierce off the track as on, and we didn't remain innovators for long. We started losing more and more races. The sponsorships dried up. Our best drivers left. There were fewer contracts with automotive companies. Even our supply business was flagging. I dumped everything we had into research and development, convinced that we could rally the business if we could just find the next big breakthrough, like the old days. But my best minds had trickled away, headhunted by competitors, I lost sponsors, government regulations ramped up, and before long, it was all we could do to keep up with the latest innovations and refinements, let alone discover any of our own. It was all we could do to even qualify for the best races."

"So, what happened then?" the same woman pressed for more details.

"Then, a mutual friend introduced me to William. A racing fan himself, he was full of ideas and excitement, and he wanted to use racing to promote a number of businesses he was working on. That was all well and good—I was in desperate need of sponsors—but I had to ask him why he wanted to sponsor Sacramento. We hadn't won a race in ages. There were a dozen other teams he could have gone with. We spoke at length about it, and he went on about Sacramento's history, how we'd helped the local racing community, and on and on. But I'll sum it up with something he said I'll never forget. 'People love an underdog.'"

A ripple of laughter ran through the small gathering. I'd heard this story a number of times from William, but it was fascinating hearing it from Don's perspective.

"That holds doubly true when there's a race involved," Don continued with a smile. "But what I thought would be a simple, straightforward sponsorship turned into more than I could have ever hoped for. Especially in the first year, William moved heaven and earth for Sacramento. He got me additional sponsors, implemented a bunch of fancy marketing that really raised our profile, and most importantly, he introduced me to a whole new generation of talent. In a matter of months, I had a new team manager, crew chief, and several of our original engineers who had helped us win in the past—all who wanted nothing more than for Sacramento to succeed."

Don chuckled. "And for the next two years, we failed. Far more often than we succeeded, anyway. The competition was just that good. And though we were a lot more financially stable than we had been in recent years, I remember feeling very tired. The team was still determined, but I admit I started thinking that maybe my racing days were done. It's not that winning was the reason I loved racing—though that's certainly a part of it. It was my unwillingness to admit defeat that stole that love away. As the saying goes, hitting yourself in the head with a hammer only hurts if you don't stop. And I felt my time had come to stop."

Another ripple of nervous laughter spread through the group. "Oh dear. What happened," someone asked.

"I could think of no better owner than William, so I approached him about buying Sacramento—the engine design and manufacturing, the racing team, the racing supply, the whole kit and kaboodle. Much to my surprise, he refused. And quite adamantly, going so far as to argue against my leaving racing at all. More than a few long conversations were had over subsequent weeks, all of which I'll again sum up. William told me that hitting yourself in the head with a hammer only hurts until the hammer breaks."

Another ripple of laughter, this time I knew they were nodding their heads at William's familiar brand of wisdom. "Where I rejected my unwillingness to admit defeat, William thrived on it. Even with a lifetime in racing, I've never met a person so unwilling to lose. It's not that the word is absent from his vocabulary. He just believes it to be a concept that nearly all of us have gotten wrong. Losing is more than a learning opportunity, more than a roadblock on the way to success. It's an integral part of success. In a weird way, it's the only way to know that you're doing everything right. By figuring out what doesn't work, you move closer to what does. You can't build a faster car without first building a slower one. And you can't build a slow car until you've first built one that starts. During those first two years, William welcomed every failure—and in hindsight, I strongly suspect he expected them, even looked forward to them. He always told us that the important thing was to keep moving forward. 'Sitting in neutral is going backwards,' he used to say. I think William succeeds because even his losses are wins."

"That sums up William to a tee," a tall gentleman in an elegant charcoal tuxedo enthused.

Dan nodded again. "And so, I stuck with Sacramento. It took two more years for that hammer to break over my skull but break it did. Inch by inch, our team got better, our engineering got better, we moved up the leaderboards, sponsors and contracts started coming in, and over the past twenty years, Sacramento has not just regained its former glory, but has clawed its way to the very top of the racing world. One of our engines even won the Indy 500 in 2001. All thanks to that mad hatter, William."

A murmur of appreciation went up as a I moved in to shake Don's hand. "What a wonderful story, Don, thanks so much for sharing. I'm Meredith Vega, we briefly met some years ago."

"Yes, of course," Don remarked. "William's young protégé. Rumor is he'd be lost without you these days."

"Oh, I'm sure he'd be just fine. Helen can manage him far better than I ever could. Say, Don, I need to commandeer the sitting room. Mind lending a hand?"

"Not at all," he said, raising his voice to address the room. "Your attention please, ladies and gentlemen. Our kind host Meredith has a brief announcement."

"Good evening, everyone, I hope you're enjoying yourselves." I waved in the servers peeking from the hallway. "I'm afraid we need to prepare the drawing room for the birthday toast. In order to tempt you away, I've brought a selection of our chef's finest hors d'oeuvres, along with some nonalcoholic sparkling wine of course, as per our host." Hushed laughter rippled through the gathering. Most everyone knew of the running joke.

"Very well, Meredith, we know when we're not wanted," Don said, putting on a dramatic air, prompting more laughter from the small crowd. "Come, everyone, let us voice our displeasure on the veranda. The setting sun shall hear of this injustice."

Don gave me a wink as the gathering followed him out, the servers trailing behind. I called Emily as a footman placed the velvet rope at the entrance. "The south drawing room is clear."

"Thanks, Meredith. The coats are on their way."

***

Making my way back to the ballroom, William caught my eye, waving me over. He stood surrounded by over a dozen partners from the firm.

"Tim, Susan, good to see you," I said, nodding to the two most senior partners under William. "Enjoying the party?"

"Of course, Meredith, it's quite the celebration," Tim said. He gestured to the man at his left. "We were just congratulating young Dominic here on making junior partner."

"Well deserved, Dom," I said. "Between your track record and the number of clients you've brought in, it was only a matter of time."

"Thank you, Meredith," Dom said, smiling from ear to ear.

"Susan, I had a chance to look over the Julian case before leaving the office today," I said. "I found something that should help."

"Oh, wonderful," she replied. "Thanks for that. I've felt like we've been missing something for a while now."

"Which one is Julian?" William asked.

"The wrongful death involving Premble Transport," Susan replied.

"Ah, yes," William said. "Tell me about it."

"Driving back to Sacramento from a stay at Lake Tahoe, the client and her husband slammed into the back of a semi parked on the side of a remote stretch of Route 50, southwest of Lake Tahoe," Susan said. "She suffered minor injuries, but her husband died on the way to the hospital. Both were wearing their seatbelts. The accident occurred shortly after midnight. The client was driving, and she stated that the truck had no safety lights. There was no warning whatsoever. The truck driver, who made regular runs between Denver, Colorado, and Sacramento, with a stop in Lake Tahoe, admitted he had pulled over for safety, opting to catch some sleep on the side of the road instead of trying to make it to Placerville, less than ten miles to the west. The CHP cited him for that non-emergency violation, as well as the lack of required warning signals for oncoming drivers. There's a good argument for negligence, but then it gets interesting. The driver claims his electronic device log had malfunctioned earlier that day, and he had yet to fill out a paper log by hand."

"So, there was no way to readily verify how long he'd been driving," William mused. "Convenient."

Susan nodded. "And given the prevalence of commercial transport companies playing fast and loose with safety regulations, often pushing their drivers to exceed their limitations and the law, it's possible that Premble Transport is liable as well. It looks like the driver was pushed to the very brink of exhaustion, hence the reason he pulled over in the middle of nowhere. What we were trying to determine was if Premble had a hand in that exhaustion. They let the driver go after the accident, which is no surprise, but they were forthcoming during discovery, turning over employee records and the driver's hours of service logs for the past six months. But we didn't find anything out of the ordinary—not a single violation. The law requires drivers to use paper logs until their electronic logs can be repaired, so we only have that for the hours leading up to the accident. At the very least, we have the driver on negligence, but Premble itself looks above board."

"I wouldn't say that," I told her. "I found something in the driver's hours of service logs. Each log is signed by the driver's immediate supervisor. In the most recent two months' worth of logs, two different signatures appear—that of the current supervisor, and that of the previous supervisor. The previous supervisor left Premble over six months ago."

Susan gasped. "They doctored the logs."

"It appears so," I nodded. "From what I can see, it could be a pattern of replacing logs that show violations with historical logs free of violations. They just failed to update the signatures. Premble has around a hundred trucks in its fleet. There's no telling how widespread this practice is."

William laughed. "Spoliation of evidence. That will at least get us a stay in proceedings until Premble turns over the real records, assuming they have them."

"And Meredith's discovery proves that Premble violated California's negligent hiring, supervision or retention law, making them directly liable," Susan added. "I'll file a motion for leave to amend the complaint, naming Premble in the suit. Meredith, you're the best. How did we miss the signatures?"

I shrugged. "It's an easy oversight."

"That's our Meredith," William said. "Ever observant, always homing in on what the rest of us miss. Well done, my dear."

"We should interview as many current and past employees of Premble as we can," Tim said. "Depending on how fraudulent and abusive the company is, we could have a class action suit on behalf of the employees, here."

Susan sighed. "I suppose, but I don't hold out much

hope. A lot of truckers protect their employers, no matter how abusive. They have bills to pay and don't want to risk losing their jobs. I doubt more than one or two would be willing to step forward."

"Ah," William said, raising a finger, "but that's an opportunity we can't pass up. What's our motto?"

"Above all, serve the client," the partners said in unison, chuckling. The principle was drilled into each of our heads from our first day at the firm.

"Exactly right," William said with a knowing smile. "Though these employees aren't yet our clients, it's our duty to do everything we can for them. And that includes showing them that they need not live under the thumb of an abusive employer. Between Premble's actual records and the interviews with employees—especially former employees—we'll be able to determine if there's a company culture devoted to taking advantage of the drivers. If that proves to be the case, then we must show them that we're here to give them a voice. We're here to show them that their best interest matters, and we can help them get compensated for their poor treatment."

He looked us each in the eye, holding our gaze as he spoke. "Collins and Associates is known throughout California and the country for going to any lengths to serve our clients. Let us never waver in that endeavor."

CHAPTER
7

Returning to the ballroom, I noticed a small gathering around Madison Avery. Somewhere in her sixties, she was an icon of the lifestyle industry, and one of the most famous people in attendance. She broke into a smile when she saw me approach. "So good to see you, Meredith," she said as we exchanged cheek kisses. "We were just discussing the human element of business—for some reason, one of the easiest aspects to neglect."

"Quite right," David Summers chimed in, a big player in cloud computing services. "I often wonder how many good people slipped between my fingers because I was too focused on the business. Was it much the same in the nineties, Madison? Before the internet and all that?"

"Absolutely," Madison replied. "I think it's the same no matter the era—pre-industrial, post-industrial, and now digital. There's something about human nature that causes us to lose sight of each other. Thankfully, we have people like William to show us the error of our ways. He always says to look five to ten years down the road. Once you can see that—which he seems to see quite well—then success is yours."

She moved her glasses up the bridge of her nose with the tip of her finger. "My first magazine was a great success through the late eighties and early nineties, expanding throughout North and South America, then Europe, Australia, and parts of Africa and Asia. Cooking, interior design, advice on childrearing and balancing career and family, we covered a lot of topics near and dear to women everywhere. A daytime talk show followed in '95, and that's when things really took off. Cooking segments, guest interviews, and audience Q&As allowed us an even wider range of discussion, giving us valuable insight into what was on women's minds. We led daytime for eight years in a row, and it was one of the best times of my life."

"It sounds amazing," David encouraged her to continue.

"But I'll always wonder how much better it all could have been if I'd had the right mindset. Like William, I grew up in humble surroundings. But unlike William, I thought success would secure my happiness. At each stage of my career, at each goal I set, I assured myself that the fulfillment I was looking for lay just around the next bend. But with every achievement came the same thing—another goal, another plan, another period of doing whatever it took to realize it. All in the vain hope of reaching this carrot I'd placed before myself. Don't get me wrong—the hard work was rewarding, and there's a lot to be said for achieving your goals. I'd built the life I'd always wanted, as far from poverty and scarcity as I had ever dreamed, but there was always something missing. Always a vague feeling of disappointment as I looked around, searching for something I didn't understand, but something I was sure I would recognize once I found it."

"I think we can all relate to some degree," I interjected.

"Unfortunately, this approach to my career put my goals first and family and people second. I wasn't a horrible leader or anything—I treated my people well, paid them well, and made a great many friends along the way. But the emotion of my work always carried a caveat. How I felt about people was inextricably tied to how they affected my success. There's nothing wrong with appreciating those who are remarkably good at what they do, but for me, there was a strong undercurrent of self-centeredness to it. And not just my peers and colleagues—every guest, every book tour, every interview I gave, every article written about me, all of it was too focused on one main concern—how does this further my goals?"

When no one interrupted she continued with a casual wave of her hand. "After over a decade of this, the world saw me as the epitome of success, while I felt somehow hollow. Thinking there was something fundamentally wrong with me, I pursued therapy, lifestyle changes, new approaches to my work and personal life, all with the same results—sooner or later, I reverted back to tried and true ways of doing things. For some reason, it was always me, me, me."

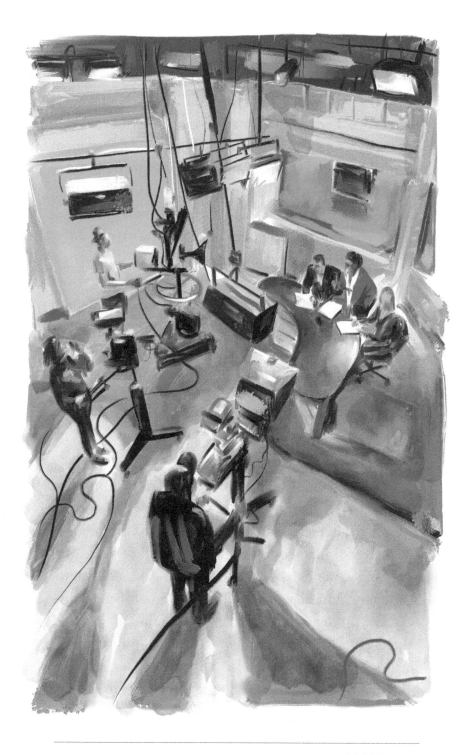

"That doesn't sound like you at all, Madison." I watched as her face transformed into a wistful smile.

"Then one day, while working on a new segment of the show called Inspirational People, my producer showed me an article about this man named William Collins. Having climbed the heights of the legal world, he moved into automotive, construction, technology, consumer goods, and a variety of other industries, making waves wherever he went. Wildly successful, of course, but it was what he left in his wake that made him memorable. People looked up to him, were inspired by him, in ways I'd never even come close to approaching. He was an entirely different kind of leader, and I wanted to learn more. Sadly, part of my reaction was tied to my estimation that he would be wonderful for the new segment of my show. You see?"

The gathering chuckled.

She forged on. "That's how deeply rooted this flaw of mine was. I couldn't escape it. Though I will say that part of me understood that my interest in him went much deeper than personal gain. For the first time, after years of searching, I felt that I may have found someone who could help me, and maybe mentor me. Anyway, my producer reached out to him, and he was kind enough to appear on the show. It turned out to be the most-viewed episode that season, which is no surprise, but what changed my life was the dinner he invited me to that evening. After the taping, I shared a few of my concerns with him, asking him what it was I was missing. He told me, 'That is a conversation best had over dinner. Join my wife and I tonight. I think I know what's troubling you.'"

"Now that sounds like William," David added.

"Over dinner, he started by asking me a litany of questions, and I soon picked up on a pattern—none of them had anything to do with me specifically, but my staff and colleagues and peers. He seemed more interested in them than he was in me. I was a bit bewildered at first, wondering when we were going to get to the heart of the discussion. But as his questions continued, growing more specific all the time, I began to have fewer and fewer answers. Before long, I only had one answer left—I don't know. Where did my producer go to school? Was she interested in starting a family, or was she a happy bachelorette? Where did she vacation, and why? What shows or segments did we disagree on, and why? Where did she see the show in five years? Helen too pressed me with questions, on and on, and concerning many others besides my producer. How many interns did I have? What were their names and aspirations?"

She looked around studying the faces around her. "Can I take a moment to talk about William's way with names?" A ripple of agreement went through the gathering.

"I'll say," David agreed. "Some ten years ago, I ran into him at a convention, a few years after having quite a similar conversation with him. He immediately asked about Jacob and Selena, two project managers of mine who went on to form their own startup. It took me a moment to even remember who he was talking about. Uncanny with names, a photographic memory or something."

"Exactly," Madison said. "And I'm convinced that he remembers names so easily because he actually cares about the people behind those names. Though I will say in his old age, he's forgetting things. But still, in most ways, he's sharp as a tack. But at that age, I should be that good!" The crowd nodded their agreement as she continued. "So, they're asking me these questions, and I begin to realize that it's intentional. They were breaking my obsessive focus on myself and forcing me to see the people around me. Not just their roles, and how their roles affected my career, but the actual *people*. Smiling, I said, 'This conversation isn't about me, is it?' And William replied, 'Only indirectly. You're gauging your success by the wrong unit of measurement. It is those around you who have made you who you are. And it is those same people who are most deserving of your attention—not yourself. You, my dear, are going to be fine. The hard work of a great many people has assured it. What you're missing, what you've been searching for all this time, is the opportunity to return the favor. And those opportunities are all around you. Your success is measured by people. Not profit, not awards or accolades, not some past or future achievement. By people, always. Though there are some who won't like you, who will disagree with you no matter what you do. And while such things are troubling at times, it's part of life. You cannot please everyone. Just be sure not to freeze up the minute you're criticized. Keep moving. When you're successful, you become a target. So, look at it as a positive. Why? Because if you weren't doing something right, they wouldn't care.' I know I'm rambling but that's exactly how I remember it. William always said, 'I invest in people first, business second when looking at acquiring any business.' And he looks at who's running it first."

Another murmur of agreement went through the gathering. "That dinner changed my life. It was like a switch had been flipped in my brain, and I saw everything in a brand-new light. I started asking questions instead of giving orders. I began listening in order to learn, instead of listening in order to respond. I began understanding who these people were, who had dedicated their careers to helping me succeed. And I found what appears obvious to us now but was sorely absent from me for far too long—they had hopes and dreams, ideas and plans, fears and concerns. They were *people*. And that realization made all the difference to me."

She paused to take a sip from her glass. She mused, "A quiet intern had a brilliant idea for a new segment. We developed it with her, and it was a hit. An associate producer had dreams of a show with an on-location format, mixing journalism and daytime talk in a way that had never been done before. We helped him develop it over the next few years, and he became the host. It's still in production today, with a viewership in the tens of millions across dozens of countries. Countless other examples over the past twenty-odd years, all thanks to that dinner. And as for me, this approach to my work and my life absolutely was the missing piece. Just as William likes to say, 'I'm always happy where I am in life, but never content.' And every day I wake up, I wonder who I'll meet today, and how I might be able to help them." She held up a finger. "I'm still terrible with names, though."

The crowd laughed, offering a scattering of applause. My phone buzzed a text in my pocket, and I nodded goodbye to Madison as the conversation continued.

Walking away, I read Emily's text. *They landed 10 minutes ago. ETA west drawing room momentarily.*

Thanks, on my way, I texted back.

I spotted William and Helen near the hearth, catching up with old friends. They were discussing the book William wrote several years ago about growing up in their small town and reminiscing about how the local fire department had been named after his late father many years ago. Approaching the edge of the gathering, I caught Helen's attention, waving her over.

"They just landed," I informed her. "I'm going to get them now. Shall we follow up with the next few surprises at the gift table?"

"Yes, absolutely," Helen said. "This is so exciting! I'll peel him away from the guests and get him to the table before you return."

I laughed, glad to see her so happy. "Wonderful, give me ten minutes or so."

I made my way back to the west drawing room, taking a more direct approach this time. There in the drawing room stood my mother, brother, and sister, a server offering them drinks from his tray. They broke into cheers when they saw me, throwing their arms wide as we embraced in a group hug.

"Meredith, you look gorgeous," my mother said, holding me away to take in my dress.

She wore a long gown of deep purple, almost black. "You too, Mom. Wearing your favorite color, I see. You look lovely."

"Not bad, Merry," my brother said, his tuxedo's modern cut giving him a stylish look. "But you're lucky I didn't wear my teal tux. Would have put you to shame."

"Marco, still trying to outdo your big sister?" I laughed, giving him a hug. "I thought we were past that."

"He still hasn't forgiven you for beating him at

Mortal Kombat all those years ago," my sister teased, giving me a hug.

"Charlotte, I love your hair," I said, fixing the dark, curling locks framing her face. Her sheer lavender gown almost glittered in the light. "It goes perfect with the dress."

"Thanks," she said, "but I'll be needing your dress after tonight. I have a wedding next week, and I want to show up the bridal party."

"Yes, yes, we're all beautiful," Marco said. "Where's the food?"

"Sorry, bro," I said, "food is for winners. Everybody knows Scorpion never beats Sub-Zero."

My mother tsked. "You kids and your video games."

We reached the ballroom several minutes later, finding William seated in a highbacked chair in front of the gift table, Helen at his side. The dance floor had been cleared, and the quartet played something low and pleasant in the background. Moving through the crowd, my family in tow, I led them to the dance floor, catching William's attention. I stood to one side, waving an arm toward my family, laughing as William's jaw dropped.

"You said you couldn't make it, you rascals!" he shouted, startling some of the guests. He leapt from his chair and Helen followed, meeting us halfway across the dance floor.

"You think we'd miss your seventy-fifth birthday?" my mother asked as they shared a hug.

My heart swelled with the knowledge that this was the crowning moment for William. He was all about family.

"We got here as soon as we could," Marco told Helen, embracing her. "Mom's flight was delayed in Chicago."

"Nonsense," Helen assured him. "We're just glad you're here. It's been too long."

"It sure has," Charlotte agreed, hugging Helen and William both.

Maggie and Bill rushed onto the dance floor, arms wide open. "Okay," Bill said, clapping his arms around Marco. "Who was in on it? Who knew?"

I laughed, waving my hands. "It was me, just me. No one else."

Maggie peered at her mother over Charlotte's shoulder. "Mom? Out with it. There's no way you didn't know."

Helen shrugged, waving a dismissive hand. "Perhaps a little bird made mention of it, I don't recall."

"Well, this is just perfect," William said, embracing Charlotte again. "It's all I could have hoped for. Come, have you eaten? Bill, Maggie, bring the grandkids around."

"There they are now," Helen said as Jason, Scott, Eric, and Emma made their way through the crowd and onto the dance floor, hugging my mother and siblings. "But William, we need you back in your seat for a few minutes."

"What for?" he complained. "Everyone's here!" Helen prodded him toward his seat. "Oh, fine. Can we at least get some more chairs? I want everyone close."

"I got it," I said, moving for the service entrance to the kitchen. "Hang tight."

Controlled chaos ensued on the other side of the double doors. I moved to the side, out of everyone's way, and watched Emily go about her work. A finger on her earpiece, phone and tablet it hand, she gave directions through the mic while gesturing a server forward. A footman hovered nearby, waiting to speak to her.

"Grab two servers, no trays, and head to the gift table," she told the server. "It looks like William wants Meredith's family with him. Get them some chairs from nearby tables." She turned to the footman. "Yes?"

"Thomas is on his way with the sparkling apple juice, but the service elevator is stuck."

"There are two flatbed carts in the back hallway," Emily instructed. "Take three more footmen and carry them downstairs. Use them to transport the cases of juice to the north service elevator and up to the main floor. Whatever you do, be careful with them. Take your time. We won't be pouring right away. What's most important is they get here in one piece."

As the footman gave a short nod and left, Emily noticed me and flashed a smile. "What's up?"

"How many hitches and snafus have you not brought to my attention tonight?" I asked her.

"Oh," she said, shaking her head, "just a few. . . dozen."

I laughed. "Remind me to give you a raise."

Her eyes lit up. "Done!"

"We're ready for the present, followed by the cake."

"Everything's ready," she said. "Chef and three helpers will cut the cake. Dishes and silverware are prepped."

"Wonderful, let's do it."

Emily tapped her earpiece. "Cue happy birthday."

Heading back into the ballroom, the string quartet started playing Happy Birthday. The conversation lulled as everyone paused, looking to William and his new guests at the gift table. From my spot off to the side, an arm around my sister, I watched him glance around the room, smiling, wondering what was next. Helen leaned close, whispering something, and he laughed. A moment later, two footmen appeared at the edge of the dance floor, pulling a flatbed cart with a large white box wrapped in a giant red bow. Cheers and applause went up as William pulled the bow, causing the four sides of the box to collapse outward. There upon the cart sat two yellow lab puppies, yawning and blinking at the light. The crowd melted as William bent low, tears in his eyes, to scoop them up. Their tails wagged as they licked his face, and the guests broke into applause.

Right on cue, Emily released Vim and Vigor. Laughter rang out as they bounced across the dance floor and over to William, more excited about the puppies than he was. Helen gestured to the extended family, and their children crashed across the dance floor like a tidal wave. From toddlers to middle-schoolers, they laughed and squealed as they crowded around William and his puppies. William let two of the older kids each take a puppy, and dozens of little hands made for their soft coats and wagging tails as Vim and Vigor barked with excitement.

As the cart was wheeled away, another replaced it, this one laden with a multi-tiered cake just like the one from the play, minus the flashing, colored lights. Far wider than it was tall, its white frosting lined with red, the Collins family crest repeated along the bottom tier. The crowd started singing Happy Birthday, their voices drowning out the quartet. Two lit candles in the shape of a seven and a five, dwarfed by the cake itself, sat before William. As the song came to an end, he blew out the candles with tears in his eyes, and thunderous applause followed.

Soon the cake and presents were behind us, and the celebration was drawing to a close. William announced to the room that we would all be moving to the veranda shortly for a toast, and to continue with the evening while final preparations were made. He then gathered the family close.

"I wanted to take a moment to thank you all for such a wonderful evening," he said, an arm around Helen.

"Having everyone together again is all I could ever want. I am immensely proud of each and every one of you. You are all quite the legacy, indeed."

CHAPTER
8

A short time later, while chatting with Bill and several guests, Doc rolled up to us in his wheelchair, pushed as always by his faithful assistant. Not many of the guests knew about Doc, and I had spent the evening smiling at their curious looks, bending close to each other to inquire about the old Japanese man snapping pictures with the classic Pentax K1000 camera looped around his neck.

"Excuse me," Doc muttered in a low, raspy voice. "Can I take a picture, please? If you could all gather together."

"No problem, Doc," Bill replied. "Bring it in, folks."

The small group gathered as Doc lifted the camera to his eye with shaky hands. He snapped multiple shots, using his thumb on the lever to wind the film forward with each one.

"Thank you" he said. "What a handsome young group." His assistant turned his chair with a smile and wheeled Doc away.

The group stood silent for a moment, sharing perplexed glances and polite smiles.

"Dad insisted that Doc be here to take some photos of the celebration," Bill explained. "I'm sure you've seen a few professional photographers hovering about throughout the evening, but those are for the local media. Doc holds a special place in Dad's heart." The group gathered closer, intrigued. "When dad was in high school, just another country boy working hard on the fruit farm, he would bring up Doc whenever he heard family or friends complain about a rough day or any kind of unfair treatment. You see, Doc was a very young boy when the Japanese bombed Pearl Harbor. He and his family, all Japanese Americans, local peach and plumb farmers all their lives, were taken off their farm and shipped out to concentration camps in Nevada. Soon after, Doc got a debilitating disease while in the camp and they couldn't help him. As a result, he was paralyzed from the waist down. All this happened while his family was being held."

"I never knew that part of the story," I looked at William for confirmation.

"Doc used to sit on the porch of his little home in the tiny, little town and wave to people as they walked by. He was an amazing guy. Doc became a symbol of charity and giving. He never complained about his circumstances. He never complained about what his family had endured—not the incarceration or the temporary loss of their farm. He lost himself in the service of others. He would show up to high school sporting events in his wheelchair, snapping photos. Days later, he'd approach each kid and give them glossy black-and-white photos as a keepsake, asking nothing in return. He would sit on his porch and wave to everyone who drove by. Struggling students and people in need would come and sit with him on his porch, sharing their troubles and receiving words of consolation and wisdom. Doc had a reputation for being a great listener."

Bill cleared his throat, his eyes blinking rapidly. "And just like Dad's childhood family and friends, my siblings and I grew up hearing about Doc whenever we complained. Dad would never let us get away with it. He reminded us of what Doc had been through, and how the man had never let that diminish the good he could bring to the world. Dad never told us why they called him Doc, but he let every one of us kids know who Doc was—a kind, giving American patriot who always looked at the positive, who chose never to complain about the unfairness of life. Dad has a collection of Doc's photos that he took of him playing sports." Bill raised his glass, and the group followed, some wiping their eyes. "The man's a heck of a photographer." After a sip of sparkling cider, he smiled. "Well, let's keep this party going."

A tap on the shoulder turned me around. Victor stood before me, as if appearing from thin air. Even taller than William, despite a subconscious hunch to his shoulders, he cut quite the dashing figure in his traditional tuxedo with white pocket square.

"You made it!" I gave him a hug, along with a few encouraging pats on the back. Though he'd been busy tracking the latest developments of the virus, his tardiness was by design—he didn't like large gatherings.

"I got here a while ago," he replied, bowing low to hug me back. "I kept running into people I know."

"Hear any good stories about William?" I asked.

"Of course," he replied. "Some sounded familiar."

I arched an eyebrow at him. "Feel like sharing?"

He glanced at the group, hesitant.

"There aren't many."

"Why not?" he said, "It'll be good for me."

"Wonderful," I turned to the group. "Everyone, I'd like to introduce Victor Forsythe, founder of Forsythe R&D. Some of you may know him best as the architect of the Net 30 online payment system."

"Oh, yes." one of the guests chimed in. "I recall reading that article about you in Collins Quarterly." Several in the crowd nodded, eyes expectant.

"Continuing the evening's tradition," I said, "I thought you might like to hear from another person William has helped in some remarkable ways. Victor?"

"Hello," he said, giving a short wave before shoving his hand in his pocket. "Yes, I met William about twelve years ago in Houston." I tapped his elbow, our signal that he needed to speak up. He cleared his throat, coming back stronger. "I was a bit of a serial college student, having finished a masters in both computer science and mechanical engineering by my early thirties, and by the time I met William, I had recently left a wonderful position at a prominent research and development firm. It was my fourth or fifth such position in about as many years, all of which I walked away from." He paused, shuffling his feet. "Are you sure you want to hear this?"

"Absolutely," Bill encouraged.

"My wife had recently left with our two children, and I certainly don't blame her. She'd finally reached the limit of her patience with me. We'd met early on in college, getting married after she graduated. Things were great for a while, but they became increasingly hard for her. I was, without question, the source of that hardship. It would be many years before I would discover the truth, which was that from childhood, I'd suffered with chronic anxiety and depression. But she loved my studious, solitary nature, always supportive of me, even when I was low. Yet even with her amazing support, my conditions kept worsening. It's funny, it's like growing older or gaining weight." He patted the small protrusion of his belly. "You never notice it as it happens. You just look in the mirror one day and think, 'Goodness, who is that? I'm far worse off than I thought I was.' So it was with me, over many such looks in the mirror throughout my entire life."

He took in a deep sigh and closed his eyes briefly. "My anxiety leans more toward the social variety—present company excluded. You people are wonderful." The crowd chuckled, easing the ever-present hunch in his shoulders. "I don't know how I made it through all the classes and group projects of college, to be honest. Well, that's not true. The alcohol helped a great deal, though thankfully, I was always able to save it for the evening. It's like the anxiety would build higher and higher throughout the day, and only afterward would I engage that pressure-release valve. Drinking helped me get over the anxieties of the day, though how I retained anything from my evening studies remains a mystery. My wife—girlfriend, at the time—didn't like that I drank alone, but she understood that it helped me get by. She was all for a few drinks from time to time, but under much more normal circumstances, like on the weekends, surrounded by friends. She was always prodding me to go out and join her, and I declined far more often than I accepted."

"Go on, Victor," I said in a soft voice.

"After she graduated, we married and had our daughter while I continued school. I'd held a vague hope that the stability of getting married and having children would snap me out of it, help me appreciate how fortunate I was, but the anxiety and depression and drinking only worsened." He held up his glass. "Sparkling apple juice, by the way. Just like William." The audience chuckled as he continued. "They call it self-medication, and it's a far more common thing than you may believe. I was using alcohol to manage my symptoms, not fully realizing just how much worse the booze was actually making me. It was an insidious cycle, driving me deeper into darkness and fear. But apparently, I'm a good actor. I finished my second degree with honors and was immediately offered a project management role at a prestigious R&D firm. And there, I excelled, helping develop new systems and programs that earned me high praise and a sterling reputation. The dichotomy is so strange because I'd long stopped caring about my work. I was just going through the motions. Part of me was sure that my peers would see the error of their thinking and recognize me for the fraud that I was, but such developments never arose. My wife was the only one who knew the darker truth."

He glanced around and grabbed a chair before taking a seat.

"Through those years at that first firm, all my side projects at home grew cobwebs—fascinating ideas I pursued in my off time became stale and uninteresting. I came to understand my plight more fully, becoming convinced that I could reason my way out of it. The alcoholism—what they're starting to call 'alcohol use disorder,' a much more accurate and informative term—was a fairly straightforward issue. I was thoroughly addicted, both physically and psychologically, but there were plenty of proven approaches to solving it. All I needed was the courage to face that particular demon. I was far more obsessed with the cause of the drinking—the anxiety and depression. I was certain that if I could just understand their cause, how they manifested, why certain bouts were so dangerously acute and hopelessly unending, then I could formulate a plan that would see me clear of them—and indeed, see me clear of mental illness altogether."

He leaned forward and folded his hands in his lap. I watched in fascination as he gathered the courage to finish his story.

"I soon walked away from my position at the firm, hopping from one position to the next over subsequent years, all the while still convinced I could think my way out of my problems. At best, I was an odd duck to my superiors and colleagues, finding further employ only via what remained of my reputation and a few kind referrals. My marriage grew increasingly strained. My wife begged me to get help. We had two kids by this point, and I was more a stranger to them than a father. I began to realize that if things kept on as they were, my wife was going to leave. And for the life of me, I couldn't tell if I cared."

He slapped his knee and stood again.

"So, I enrolled in a sixty-day rehab center. Therapists aren't interested in discussing mental illness when there's addiction present, insisting that the addiction be addressed if there's to be any hope of resolving the underlying mental issues, and I can see why. Those two months were profoundly transformative. I'd no idea how slow and foggy my mind had become, how absolutely snowed under with unnamed grief I'd been, like a giant weight upon my shoulders. I emerged a renewed man, ready to take on the world. I reconnected with my family, continued therapy and meds, and soon found a new position at a great firm. Things were looking better than they had in years."

I walked over and pressed a light hand on his shoulder. "Go on Victor. We want to hear the rest."

He nodded. "But after a year or so of continuous therapy and riding the medication roller coaster, working with my therapist to find the right combination with the least side effects, I experienced little improvement. My heart still wasn't in my work. I was spending less and less time with my family. The novelty of sobriety wore off, replaced by the familiar reality of a malfunctioning mind, and I realized with horror that the weight I thought I'd left behind at rehab had never disappeared, only diminished. I soon left that firm as well, holing up in my workshop at home, avoiding my family. Alcohol had always been my only relief, and it wasn't long before I was once again ankle-deep in empty cans and bottles, trying to find something in life to cling to." He wiped an unseen tear from his eye.

"My wife demanded I leave, and I was too lost to argue. I had a small apartment for a while, until the divorce papers arrived. It broke my heart, but I signed over custody of the kids. The house as well—I certainly had no use for it. A year later, she sold the house and moved closer to family in New York. I stopped caring altogether, and soon I was on the street—no job, no car, no reason to go on."

Victor straightened up almost to full height and looked straight at William.

"Some months later, I was approached by a private investigator. A man named William Collins wanted to meet me for lunch. He'd pay for a week's stay at a motel and give me five hundred dollars in cash if I'd give him one hour of my time. Desperate for a drink, not even remembering when I'd last had a hot shower, I accepted. We met the following day at a local diner. He had acquired a company that had developed some early concepts of mine into a rather advanced AI. Impressed with my work, he'd spent some time piecing my career together, following a breadcrumb trail of accomplishments up to the point I'd fallen off the map. He then hired a PI, who was able to track me down to my little spot in Houston's underbelly."

William nodded in understanding encouraging the man to continue.

"He wanted to ask me questions, assuring me that my payment was not contingent on my willingness to answer. He even handed me the money before our server had time to get us coffee. Not seeing the harm in it, I agreed to answer what I could. Something about him caused me to open up. I think it was his eyes. No judgment, no pity—just curiosity and concern. I wound up sharing far more than I'd intended, spending over our allotted hour telling him my story. He then went on to ask about my early work and the various projects I'd spearheaded. His company was on the cusp of something big, but they couldn't break through. He wanted to pick my brain about how best to approach their issues. Before long, we were in deep discussion over his team's roadblocks, what they were doing wrong, and where they should instead turn their attention." Victor chuckled, his eyes far away. "Through the shakes of alcohol withdrawal, too sick to have more than a few cups of coffee, I found myself excited about a project. It had been years since I'd felt that way. I'd forgotten what it was like.

"At one point, William held up a hand, saying, 'I'm understanding only a fraction of what you're saying, my boy. Your expertise is far beyond my own, and it certainly sounds as though you have answers that my team does not. I'd like to get you some help so that you can come work for me. But with conditions: you get sober, and you work hard. I think hard work can solve many people's problems in life. You can succeed no matter where you are on the ladder of life.' I was flattered, even a bit tempted, but I declined. I wasn't who he was looking for. I'd be able to help for a few weeks, a few months at best, but eventually I'd walk away, as I had in the past. He needed someone he could rely on. Someone that cared as deeply as he did. There were any number of talented engineers out there with far better ideas than me. And that's when I learned of Mr. Collins' inability to take no for an answer."

The gathering chuckled, sharing knowing looks. "'That's just it, Victor,' he said. 'You do care as much as I do. You've just learned to ignore it. Your talent in your chosen fields is far more unique than you know. You have a vast intellect, Victor. But there is one thing in this world it will never accomplish.' He leaned in close, his eyes drilling into mine, laying bare the darkest corners of my heart. 'You will never be smart enough to out think yourself.'"

I watched as headed nodded in understanding. We had all heard these words from William at some point in time.

"I'll never forget those words. I'd spent years believing I could think my way out of my depression and anxiety, but it was impossible. I'd never felt so free, yet so hopeless at the same time. "'And I'll tell you something else, my lad,' he said. 'None of us are smart enough. And that's as it should be. That's why there are others—to help us where we cannot help ourselves. However, helping yourself is fundamental, and you've certainly taken all the proper steps over the years to get yourself the help you need. But I think you may have forgotten one vital thing in your long search for answers. You're a fixer, like me. And there is little in this world more satisfying than fixing what is broken. But you've spent so long obsessed with fixing yourself that you've forgotten about all the other broken people in the world. And one of the best ways to help yourself is to spend time helping family and others. You are needed, my boy. There is only one of you, making you the rarest resource in all the world. And if you listen closely, you will again hear that world calling upon you now.'"

I watched at Helen smiled at William. It was a loving, all-knowing gesture.

"He was right. I was a fixer. What I'd loved about my work in the first place was its near-limitless ability to help people, to fix what was broken. My work gave me the opportunity to someday leave this world a little less broken than how I'd found it. But somehow, all of that had become lost to me in my obsession to fix myself. Mental illness, addiction—they are blinders, limiting your vision to only a small slice of your life, veiling that slice in a darkness so thorough, you forget that there's far more to this world, and far more to yourself. They deafen you, keeping you from hearing the pleas of your loved ones, ensuring you only hear what your demons want you to hear. You stop hearing the world when it calls upon you. But in that moment, I could see again. I could hear again—as clearly as you see and hear me now."

"What happened next?" someone asked.

"I accepted William's offer to set me up with an in-patient rehab. I flew out the next day and never looked back. When I got out a few months later, I led his R&D team to a minimum viable product within six months. He then let me handpick an R&D team to work on the projects of my choice. He had put me in touch with some amazing therapists, and I got back on the medication roller coaster. Within a few years, we found the right combination of meds for me. I learned that hard work also kept my mind and my body focused and away from my issues. And with that new baseline of anxiety and depression—that weight on my shoulders that was now far lighter than it had ever been—I was able to make the most of the therapy. It's truly amazing how effective therapy can be, once medication puts you within reach of understanding and implementing it. The combination of meds and counseling has been invaluable—as have William's words at that diner, so many years ago. I went on to do some wonderful work at his firm, conceptualizing and developing projects that truly helped people. Eventually, he helped me establish my own R&D firm, where we're working to solve some of the world's biggest, most fundamental problems—helping the world become a better place."

Victor nodded toward the end of the row of tables, and the group turned to see William and Helen laughing, surrounded by a large gathering. "That man saved my life. And I assure you, I'm only one of many."

CHAPTER
9

Standing at the back of the dais, I nodded to Emily at the south entrance. A silent river of servers with trays poured into the night air, mixing with the sea of burgundy umbrellas that dotted the veranda's expansive tiers below me. Strings of lanterns hung from intermittent lampposts, enveloping all in a soft glow. A mist of rain had stopped an hour ago, leaving a light breeze that ruffled the umbrellas. Some of the guests had retrieved their coats at the south drawing room on their way, with most of the women wrapped in shawls. I approached the mic, smiling to William and Helen where they sat at a table on the left side of the dais. My family sat at the nearest tables, just below us.

"Hello, everyone. On behalf of William and Helen, thank you so much for joining us to celebrate William's seventy-fifth birthday!" A wave of cheers and applause broke out. "As most of you know, I'm Meredith Vega, business partner and close friend of the Collins, and a nearly lifelong mentee of the Goose."

Calls of "Goose!" rang out across the veranda. William stood, clasping his hands together and shaking them above his head as the calls continued.

William leaned down and I heard him whisper to

Helen, "I'm uncomfortable with all this talk about me. It feels like 'this is your life'."

Helen replied, "For once, dear, enjoy the fruits of your life."

"I've heard some profound and moving stories tonight, and I know I'm not the only one. A few of you have heard my own story, though most have not, and if you'll indulge me, I'd like to share it with you now."

Another round of applause went up as I adjusted the mic. "My mother is Annabelle Vega." I smiled at her, and she beamed with pride. "Some of you may know her as the founder of The Village, one of the nation's leading daycare chains. But back in the day, she was a hardworking single mom of three. After landing a new housekeeping position at an upscale hotel in Sacramento, she came to William and Helen's rescue one night when they locked themselves out of their room, leaving one- and two-year-old Bill and Maggie trapped inside. Using her master key to open the door, they rushed in to check on the children. It had only been a few moments, so they were fine, though they were scared and crying. From Helen's arms, Maggie reached out a tiny hand for Annabelle. Helen handed the child over, and almost immediately, Maggie stopped crying. My mother explained that she had three children of her own, and had spent her youth helping raise her three younger siblings while her parents worked long hours picking crops throughout Southern California. Having debated for some time if they should hire a nanny, William and Helen decided then and there that they wanted Annabelle. Their offer far exceeded her current pay, and she was inclined to accept. However, the distance to the new Collins estate would require a car, which she didn't have, and daycare would cost more than she was paying already. They asked her to come visit on her next day off to see if they could persuade her. They even invited her to bring my siblings and me, saying they'd send a car for us and pay her a day's wages at their offered rate. Even back then, the Collins knew how to make an offer immune to refusal."

The audience broke into laughter, with a few whistles piercing the night air.

"Of course, my mother fell in love with the estate. Construction was nearing completion, and William and Helen gave us a tour, ending at one of the guest houses. They said if she accepted, it would be hers for the entirety of her employ, at no cost to her. I was only five at the time, but I remember my mother tearing up as my siblings and I ran around the place, exploring. It was easily four times the size of our little two-bedroom apartment downtown, but the guest house wasn't even the half of it. It was the estate itself—it was magical. Trees, and specifically fruit trees, as far as you could see, the lake, the open air—it was a whole different world from our dingy neighborhood of concrete and police sirens. The Collins offered to help my mother transfer us to the local school district, and just like that, four people had a brand-new life."

A round of cheers and applause went up. Helen reached for William's hand as they smiled at each other.

"We're all aware that the Collins estate is a special place, but what made growing up here such a treasure were the Collins themselves and the staff. They treated us like family, and indeed, they *are* our family. Bill and Maggie are my brother and sister. Helen is a second mom to me. And my mother is a second mom to Bill and Maggie." I gestured behind me, where Thomas and Mable stood at the south entrance. "Thomas, the revered Collins Estate butler, and Mable, the all-knowing, all-seeing keeper of the house, are my uncle and aunt. And William himself is the father I never had."

Another round of applause washed over the crowd as William blew me a kiss.

"Time flew on the estate, and as my five siblings and I made our way through elementary school, there was less call for a loving nanny. But William had his eye on another opportunity. Over those years, he came to recognize the telltale signs of a savvy entrepreneur in his midst. My mother was a quick study, and she knew a thing or two about pinching pennies to get by. The Collins could have easily provided her with another role here on the estate, but they were loath to see her passion for childcare go to waste. They could have referred her to another loving family in need of a nanny, but they instead approached her with an idea. Why provide childcare to one family when she could serve countless families across the country? William and Helen wanted to help her start her own daycare center, assuring her that we could stay at the estate for as long as we liked. A firm believer that it takes a village to raise a child, my mother founded The Village daycare center in Sacramento."

"That place has the best reputation in the whole area," a voice called out.

I nodded. "Over the next three years, my mother opened three additional centers, and within ten years, there were franchises throughout California. Today, there are nearly fifteen hundred locations across the US. And by working with government agencies at the local, state, and federal levels, each and every franchise has at least a third of their capacity reserved for low-income families. But my mother didn't stop there. She created a hiring program for parents interested in a career in childcare, providing them with training and free on-site care for their own children while they learned valuable new skills. And the most talented among these caregivers became eligible for a fast-track program that provided them with their very own franchise within five years. Like dominoes, each of these franchises offers the same program, giving low-income parents and single parents everywhere a chance at a new life."

I turned and looked at William. "As we all know,

William's reputation for producing wealth led to his moniker, The Goose. And like the Golden Goose of legend, that wealth was created consistently, steadily over time, requiring patience and forethought. But those of us here, and the countless others he's helped over the years, know that this is the lesser of its meanings. William creates far more than just wealth wherever he goes—he creates the conditions necessary for people to become their better selves. And for a very select number of us, like my mother, myself, a few of the other partners at the firm, and a few other guests, we've been given the rare privilege of the Goose's direct mentorship—out of the thousands who have sought his individual attention, it is only we fortunate few who've had access to the full breadth of his wisdom and the full depth of his care. And though I know he wishes he had the time to take on more mentees, he has still made it a priority to give his family and countless others the tools they need to lift themselves up and create the life they've always wanted. And he's instilled in us all the principles that allow us to do the same for our families and others. In this way, we are all his children."

The crowd applauded—free of cheers and whistles, it carried a reverent quality, a solemn appreciation that brought them one by one to their feet. I turned to William and Helen, applauding as well. As the ovation stretched on, Helen poked him in the arm, gesturing to the crowd. Reluctantly, William stood, offering slight bows as he waved them off. Giving up, he sat back down as the applause continued.

I raised my glass. "We spent two years planning this commemorative vintage of sparkling apple juice for tonight's celebration. It's not nearly as bold or endearing or memorable as our William, but it's a start." The crowd raised their glasses along with William and Helen. "To the Goose."

"To the Goose," the crowd said as one, sending an echo across the lake as we drank.

The audience resumed their seats, and I continued. "And now for the moment we've all been waiting for. Or at least, the moment William has been waiting for. A final present for the birthday boy." Laughter broke out as William danced in his chair. "Not to spoil the festivities with business, but it's required if I'm to hand it over—and I can think of no other crowd more interested in such talk, am I right?"

A round of cheers and whistles went up. "Let's hear it!" someone yelled, causing a ripple of laughter.

"I thought as much," I said. "William, a number of us have been working on the perfect gift. Yet it doesn't come in a box with pretty wrapping paper, nor with a bow tied neatly around it. After all, few challenges in life do. But that is exactly what life's greatest gifts tend to entail—challenge. And we have one for you unlike anything you've faced before. Last year's national peach harvest was down three percent. Hardly newsworthy, but the cause of it may be. Thought to be a typical species of the mosaic tree virus—a diverse classification of blight kept in check by a conventional series of mitigation practices—we have reason to believe it may be a novel species, and one worth a great deal of concern. Scattered reports indicate a number of locations in California where mitigation has had little to no effect. And this year's harvest reports indicate a bigger hit, with some projections putting it as high as six percent. This still appears to be little cause for concern, but after tracking the issue closely with Victor and a few others, this virus is proving extremely virulent, which likely means exponential spread before next year's harvest and beyond. Left unchecked, the results could be devastating."

No longer smiling, William had an intense look in his eyes. The crowd reflected his demeanor. "So far, it is indeed unchecked. Most everyone is still of the mind that it's a typical species, with more rigorous mitigation all that's needed to stamp it out. But we disagree. Our preliminary field tests show that the virus doesn't respond to conventional measures. Disinfectant solutions for contaminated equipment have no effect. Worse, the mites responsible for additional spread appear resistant to conventional pesticides—the virus is adapting them in some way we don't yet understand. We've replicated test results at multiple locations, with the latest coming in throughout this very evening. What's more, we've confirmed the virus in other states. Hopefully, if we can get ahead of this, we can curb exponential spread and avert disaster. But as of this moment, there remains too much we don't yet know, save this—the worst-case scenario could be dire, and I'm not just speaking of the economic impact of losing entire harvests. If the virus adapts and spreads to other fruits and vegetables, or to grain used for animal feed, the country may experience food scarcity that hasn't been seen since the Great Dust Bowl."

I paused to let that sink in.

"I know this sounds alarmist, so allow me a moment to alleviate your concerns. Chances are high that with a little experimentation, a little trial and error, we'll find new mitigation practices before next harvest, and this entire situation will barely make the news. But my colleagues and I want the best chance possible to ensure that outcome. And that means we need the Goose. William, we're working on a stack of briefs for your review. The latest metrics, locations, maps, and a running list of contacts at farms, government agencies, universities and advocacy organizations throughout every peach-producing state. Victor has his entire R&D firm at your disposal, and we're compiling a number of contract research organizations for additional manpower."

I took a few steps toward William.

"More than anything, you wished for a challenge for your birthday. Something new, something you've never experienced before." I paused, smiling. "Will this do?" A chuckle rolled through the audience as I turned to them. "And what do you say? Is the Goose up for the challenge?"

"Go get 'em, Goose!" someone yelled. The audience erupted into laughter and applause. I joined in, gesturing William toward the mic.

He rose from his seat and made his way across the dais, wrapping me in a bear hug. "Thank you, my dear," he said, squeezing me tight. "I'm so proud of you."

"Happy Birthday, Dad," I replied, squeezing him back.

He held me at arm's length, eyes wet. Seeming about to speak, he instead buried me in his arms once more.

Pulling away, I wiped his eyes with a thumb. I whispered, "Go get 'em, Goose."

Helen reached for my hand as I took William's seat. "You have William's sense of showmanship as well," she said, reaching over to embrace me in a half-hug.

"I learn from the best," I said, laughing.

William adjusted the height of the mic as the audience quieted, taking a few moments to gather himself. "My friends, I don't have the words to convey my appreciation to you for this unforgettable evening. Well, as a matter of fact I do, but the problem is it will take me a great many words to find them, so I ask that you bear with me." He cleared his throat and began.

"I've tried to spend my life, as best as I know how, following a set of principles designed to bring out the best in me. But I learned from my father, my mother, and most especially, from my lovely wife Helen, that the only way to make that happen is to help family and others bring out the best in themselves."

He blew Helen an air kiss.

"We are not alone for a reason, but there is only so much you can do to help people unless they are following up, working hard and not giving up. The best way to do good in this world, and live a meaningful life, is by enriching family and others. To quote a tired cliche 'It is better to teach a man to fish, rather than give a man a fish.'" William chuckled, scratching an ear. "You know, I always found it funny. The only reason we've survived this long is by relying on each other." He smiled at Annabelle. "As someone even more hardworking than I once told me, 'it takes a village to raise a child'. Tribes are what allowed us to survive and thrive. Communities are built by everyone chipping in for the greater good. But the more prosperous we become, the farther from that truth we stray. It's also from hard work and persistence. I'm a firm believer that money helped civilize humanity, drawing us from our huts and caves and allowing us to build empires. And here we stand, in this wonderful modern age, all our needs met, all our dreams within reach, perched on the cusp of the very stars themselves."

He gestured with a wide sweep of his hands.

"I was once asked what one thing I would change or do better in my life looking back at the last 75 years. The answer was nothing. All my failures, the things that I did wrong, the things that were not fair, all the stumbles were there to build me up to become successful. And failures become learning experiences, and then they are not failures. Remember, to get beautiful trees that bear fruit, you have to prune back every year. This builds stability so when the hard winds come and hit you, you are able to withstand them. Yes, things are fair and in balance because when others complain about not being fair, they are focusing on the negative. The successful are going to move on and not worry about what is and is not fair in life. Is it fair that some were given more money than I was growing up? Was it fair that others were smarter than me in school? Was it fair that school was easier for others than me? Was it fair that others had mentors in business, and I did not? Hard work, tenacity, learning from others, and enduring to the end are the most important things one can do to succeed."

He lifted the microphone from the stand and took a few steps forward.

"I remember speaking to some high school students and one student asked me, 'why is my father not financially successful and you are, what is the difference?' My answer was simple. I don't know your father or what he has been through but maybe, just maybe I got off the ground more times than he did?"

William pointed a finger off to the east. "Across the grounds and through the trees, just on the water, there stands a small grove of peach trees. Most of the trees are only about five years old, but one of them is nearly twenty—three times the size, and every bit as healthy and robust as the sprouts around it. Those who know peaches will tell you that tree isn't supposed to live that long. And it's certainly not supposed to still be bearing fruit. But the tree doesn't mind. It doesn't ask why. It just carries on doing what it does best, knowing that is enough."

He wagged his finger again.

"On that tree hangs a swing. As a child growing up on a peach farm, I also had a tree, and on that tree hung a swing. A kid who picked peaches all day sat on that swing in the evenings, looking out at the vast expanse of his future, imagining the possibilities. Nobody ever thought a supposedly average, small-town boy would achieve what he did. And today, an old man sits on this swing, looking back over the vast expanse of a lifetime, wishing he could tell the boy not to take a single moment for granted. The old man then looks at the ground, realizing that he's not looking back with regret. He's looking back with envy at the boy's infinite possibilities. And eventually, the old man looks out across the water, realizing that like the tree above him, he's still here. He's still strong. And he has many possibilities yet to discover."

William took a measured moment to scan all the faces and lock eyes with as many people as he could.

"And so, I will not ask why. I will instead carry on, doing what I do best. And perhaps, like the tree, that is enough. Though carrying on is made all the sweeter knowing that you are here with me, and we can carry on together."

The fireworks were spectacular, and the rain never came that night.

CHAPTER
10

The late-morning sun hidden by trees off to my left, I sat in William's swing, taking in the warm air and watching fish breach the placid water. Insects buzzed, birds called, and the stillness worked the previous night's excitement from my body.

The celebration had been a hit with the guests, and all pledged their support for whatever the peach tree virus brought to our door. After many a goodbye and the staff had buttoned up for the night, we retired. Mom, Marco, Charlotte, and I stayed the night in the guest house for old time's sake. The kids, grandkids, and most of the extended family were spread throughout guest houses and rooms at the main house.

I typically stayed at the estate for a few nights of any given month, unless I was off on an extended business trip, but having the family back together made last night special. My family and I stayed up late, catching up over leftover hors d'oeuvres and sparkling apple juice, laughing over childhood stories and reminiscing about the past. I slept better than I had in years.

I heard a shuffling off to my right, finding William making his way down the dirt path.

"I thought you'd be you here, my dear," he said.

"How'd you know?"

"You seemed pretty concerned about your findings so far with the virus."

"Was that part of the toast a little overboard?"

He scoffed. "No, of course not."

"I debated giving you the news today, in private. I didn't want to kill the mood of the party."

"No, it was the right move. There were a lot of powerful people on that veranda. It's good that they heard about it. And if it turns out to be nothing—no harm, no foul."

"I suppose." I kicked at the dirt with a toe. "I don't think it'll be nothing."

William smiled, patting me on the shoulder. "Neither do I. I just got done looking at some emails I had Victor send me. But we have to be patient. We'll know more in a few days, after they've gotten samples back to their labs for more thorough tests."

"I used to have a spot like this when I was a kid, you know."

"Really? Where?"

"The woods past the track. We found an old tire. Bill snagged some rope from one of the sheds and we made a swing. We'd come back and play from time to time, but as we got older, they seemed to forget about it. But I kept coming back."

"How come?"

I smiled. "It was this beautiful clearing. The trees

were perfect, the light was perfect, it was like my own little paradise. Your story last night reminded me of it, and I realized I spent a lot of time thinking about the same things you did as a kid. Imagining the possibilities, weighing my options, making big decisions. It was an important place. And then I realized that I haven't had a place like that in a very long time. I think it would do me good to find one."

"We should go on a hike sometime, see if it's still there."

"I don't know. I'm afraid of what I'll find. What if it doesn't look the same, and I don't even recognize it? What if we walk right through it, and I don't even know it? Or worse, what if we find it, and it doesn't feel the same? I risk spoiling my memories of it."

William inspected a peach above his head. "I think the importance of such a place justifies the risk. If that risk is even relevant."

"What do you mean?"

"By avoiding the place, you preclude yourself from making new memories. That's the secret of it. Memories are set in stone. But their creation lies in looking ahead. That's the strange thing about fearing change. You become so focused on not losing what you have, that what you really end up losing is your ability to gain everything new."

"What if you lost this place?"

He paused, considering. "The same applies, my

dear. How am I to find a new spot if I never lose my old one?"

I rose from the swing, throwing an arm around him and directing him through the trees. Toward the back of the grove, we approached the three sickly ones. I pointed to a cluster of peaches, smaller and discolored compared to the others. "See there?"

William took a closer look, rolling them around on their stems.

"And here," I said, pointing to some leaves. Spotted and wrinkly, they looked far different than normal.

"Did you tell Victor?"

"I sent him home with some samples last night. Each tree and sample labeled. He wants to send a small team to give the grove a thorough check."

"I'll talk to the groundskeeper," William said, determined. "I'm not sure if he tends them or someone on his crew. I'll warn them of the situation, and gather all their information—other farms and properties they work on, where they store their tools, a list of all fertilizers, pesticides, and other—"

I started laughing.

"What?" he said, smiling.

"I take it you've accepted this new challenge?"

"Of course! I couldn't dream of one better." He led me back to the front of the grove. "My dear Meredith. Yes, I may lose my little slice of paradise. And yes, I will mourn it. But this is the way of things. The challenge is everything. And there can be no challenge without change."

He sat me on the swing, giving me a push. I laughed as he pushed again. "Come on, swing your legs," he invited. "You know this is all I care really care about. Being here with family, enjoying my moments of solitude, just being."

I gave in, and soon I was swinging to and fro like a kid at recess. "What you must remember, my dear, is that quite often, things haven't changed *yet*. So, it's best to enjoy them while you can."

"But the virus," I said over my shoulder. "What if it changes things beyond repair? What if we can't stop it?"

William laughed, giving me another push. "Have I taught you nothing, my dear? There's no such thing as losing."

***

We made our way back to the house, and after a late breakfast with the family, we all said our goodbyes as the kids, grandkids, and extended family packed into vehicles headed for the highway or the airport. Standing at the east entrance, waving to the vehicles as they left the plaza, William shared a surprise of his own.

"Meredith, please touch base with Arnold. Ask him if our departure is on schedule."

A knowing smile played at Helen's lips. "And where are you off to now? Another business trip, I'm sure."

"Not me, sweetie," William assured her, "but we! I want to share something with you both. I need your opinions before making a decision. And Meredith, please invite your assistant Emily along. She deserves something special after all her hard work."

"Will do," I said, taking out my phone and stepping away as Helen began bombarding William with questions. "Hi Arnold, it's Meredith. How are we looking?"

"On schedule for a 12:30 departure, ma'am," Arnold replied.

"Great, thanks. Uh, where we headed, anyway?"

"Sorry, ma'am," Arnold chuckled. "William said that's classified."

I barked a laugh. "Did he, now? Thanks Arnold, we'll see you soon."

I texted Emily, who'd been given a room at the main house last night. We were planning on heading back to Sacramento together after breakfast. *Helicopter ride back postponed. Taking a side trip with William and Helen. Meet us at the east entrance.*

You got it, she texted back. *Be there shortly.*

"But are you sure a single bag will be enough, dear?" Helen was saying to William.

"Absolutely. We're not going far, and we're returning tomorrow."

"Very well," she said, sighing. "But you know I prefer to *give* surprises, not receive them."

William's eyes grew wide and innocent. "Really, sweetie? I had no idea. I do apologize."

She squinted at him, a menacing look in her eye.

"Chop, chop!" he insisted. "We mustn't be late."

An hour later, we pulled up to the jet at Truckee-Tahoe airport. The new Embraer jet sat high and sleek on the tarmac; a coiled spring ready to pounce at the sky. The dark blue of the Collins & Associates logo shined in the sun on the tail. Arnold stood at the steps leading to the cabin.

"Good to see you, Arnold," William said. "What's our flight time?"

"You too, sir," Arnold replied. "Just over an hour."

"Wonderful," William said. Arnold helped Helen up the steps, and William waved us forward. Emily was all smiles—she'd never been on a private jet before.

With seating for eleven, there was plenty of room for the four of us. We sat just ahead of the wings, with Emily and I facing William and Helen. As we leveled off some time later, heading northwest, Emily grabbed her phone. "Would it be okay if I took some pictures out the window?" she asked over the thrum of the engines.

"Of course, go right ahead," William said.

Unbuckling her seatbelt, Emily stood at the large window between her and Helen, snapping pictures.

"What do you think, so far?" William asked her.

"This is amazing!" she exclaimed. "My friends would be so jealous."

"You have social media, I assume?" William asked.

"Of course," Emily said.

William gestured at her phone. "Give it here, have a seat."

Emily complied, and William held her phone up. "Say cheese!"

"Cheese!" we said in unison.

"There," he said, handing back the phone. "Put that out there for everyone to see. And when we land, be sure to snap a few of the jet and post them as well."

"Really?" Emily said. "Thanks, I will!"

"Thank you, my dear," William laughed. "There's nothing like a bit of free advertising. Social media's been an incredible development for marketing of all kinds. Truly game-changing stuff."

No sooner had we leveled off than Arnold announced we were beginning our descent, and in no time, we were on the ground at Del Norte County Regional Airport in Crescent City. An SUV and driver awaited us, and an hour later we were traveling steep, narrow roads off Route 199, where the hills turned into mountains somewhere northwest of Klamath National Forest.

The driver took a random turn up a dirt road, and after half a mile, the trees parted to reveal a beautiful ranch. Set atop a rise overlooking a sprawling landscape of wooded hills and grassy expanses, the main house afforded a view that stretched on for miles. Large shade trees dotted the fenced-in yard, and a wide, one-story barn sat nearby, next to a corral.

"The realtor was kind enough to give us the afternoon," William said as we piled out of the vehicle and approached the house.

"It's gorgeous, William," Helen said.

"Good, I'm glad you think so," William replied. "I've grown fond of it myself. Let's take a look inside."

A two-story timber frame house with peaked roofs and a large wraparound porch, it looked as sturdy as the landscape it was built upon. An open floorplan with a modern kitchen took up the first floor, with three bedrooms on the second floor, including a master suite with a private bath.

"Wait until you see the best part," William said, leading us to the far side of the building. Opening a sliding glass door off the dining area, the porch offered a view of a large stream running through the property. Wide and winding, we could just make out the muffled rush of its waters where they glistened in the sunlight some thirty yards away.

"A little over a mile of it rests on the property, fed from the mountains to the east," William stated. "Excellent fishing, I'm told."

The four of us stood in silence, leaning against the

railing and taking it all in. The fresh air, the warm sunshine, the calls of birds and insects against the backdrop of the running water—it was a far cry from the hustle and bustle of the Collins estate.

"It's marvelous, William," Helen said. "But is it a bit small? And why now? Is this a birthday present to yourself?"

William laughed. "It's a gift for you and me, sweetie. And the occasional guest or two," he added, patting my shoulder. "It's meant to be small. I looked around at a number of bigger places, and they all reminded me of the estate. I wanted something that reminded me of my roots, out here in the country, away from the wider world and all its troubles."

"I think I get it," I said.

William arched an eyebrow. "You do?"

"This place, it's your new swing," I said. "Somewhere you can go to have some peace and quiet to think about the big decisions. You're saying that we're not always at the whim and mercy of inevitable change—sometimes, we can affect change ourselves. To some degree, often to a larger degree than we would believe, we're the captains of our own vessels. And by extension, when sad change is brought upon us, we hold the power to recover from it, even turn it into a positive." I paused, thinking. "There really is no such thing as losing."

"I couldn't have said it better myself," William said,

leaning his elbows on the railing. "And as for change, I can see it coming." He rubbed his hands together, more in an impatient way than a nervous one—he wanted to confront it.

"What do you see?" I asked.

William sighed. "When I was a child on the small farm, long before the complex insurance and virus-free certification programs and other risk-management measures seen in today's agriculture, there was a much wider margin for error—a much wider margin for tragedy. A popular nursery in our county had recently changed hands, sold to a corporation I've long since forgotten the name of. The new owners offered great prices on new trees, and they had a wide variety of cultivars. It seemed like a boon for area farmers. But the next two harvests were the worst in recent memory. It was always suspected that the new owners had adopted some rather lax policies regarding quality control and disease prevention, but before anything could be done about it, the company sold off the nursery. Dozens of farms were affected, setting families back years. Several farms were even foreclosed."

"You suspect something similar with this new virus? But it's much too big, much too widespread for it to be a man-made issue, isn't it?"

"Consolidation, my dear," William stated. "Consolidation. Fewer companies hold more power than ever before, and that includes the agriculture industry." He sighed again. "I always thought that could lead to tremendous prosperity—and sometimes it does. But far too often for my liking, it leads to corruption and willful negligence. I might be mistaken, but something doesn't sit right with this new virus. My gut is telling me something's awry. And I've learned to listen to my gut."

"What can I do?" I asked.

"You've always had an eye for investigation, Meredith," William said. "That's one of the many reasons why you're so good at business. Your observant nature leads you to facts that others don't even know they should be looking for."

He paused, watching the ribbon of blue as it splashed and sparkled in the sun. "So, first and foremost, I need you to make some inquires."

**

EPILOGUE

You have seen just a glimpse into William Collins life and what he is about and has become. However, this did not happen by chance and did not occur over a few years but occurred over decades of hard work, failing, and learning important lessons at a young age. How is it that William Collins learned such valuable lessons to become the successful businessman he had become. How was it that he learned to love peaches so much and peach orchards that generally were not good money investments?

Book two of *Goose* will be taking you back to William Collins life when he was a young boy in a small northern California country town where he grew up with very little. Though little, he was happy and enjoyed having no money and little to spend. Struggles were real and were lifelong lessons that took him from the small town to big city deals while keeping the integrity and moral compass of a country boy. Yes, God fearing, respect of your elders and calling adults Sir and women Madam were in order on the old Collins ranch where he grew up as a boy. He did not have a paper route like the normal city boys but worked in the fields for an employer at the age of 14, not to mention since 5th grade was doing the same hard manual labor on his family small farm without pay. Pay he was taught was what you received at the

dinner table, a good hot meal from his mom that was an
excellent cook.

‎‎*who*

   You as a reader will be brought back to simpler
times, not the more complicated and busy times of the
current William Collins that was the subject of the current book. You will fee euphoric as you live the life of
William as a child starting in the 5th grade. No money,
a hard working family, happiness revolved around God,
Family and close friends—friends that lived in single
wide trailers yet knew no different. Everyone was broke
so nobody knew any better. The adventures are exhila-
rating and dangerous. Puppy love is typical in a small
town where the weekends were all about continuous
work and only an occasional brief time to hang out with
friends. William attends a small town old broken down
k-8 school where the teachers were not easy and did not
care to allow children to back talk. It was a time when
students got in trouble and the parents were on the side
of the teachers. A time when a child was in trouble the
parent would show up to the school and ask the child
what they did wrong instead of coming into the school
upset at the teacher or principle for disciplining their
child. A time when the principal had a wooden paddle
with holes in it and used it as a "hearing aid" so the out
of control student could hear better if you know what I
mean.

   Come back with us and enjoy book two of *Goose*, his
younger years.

ABOUT FREDERICK W. PENNEY

 Fred Penney, Injury Lawyer® has the highest AVVO personal injury attorney rating of a 10– "Superb Lawyer". Frederick W. Penney is an AV Preeminent rated Attorney by Martindale Hubbell, one of the most prestigious ratings systems in the United States. This is the highest possible rating in both legal ability and ethical standards. Mr. Penney has also been rated AV Preeminent by the opinions of the members of the Judiciary. Frederick Penney has been appointed by the Placer County Court as a Settlement Conference Judge, better known as a Judge Pro-Tem. Mr. Penney preforms this duty only on occasion. For over 30 years Mr. Penney and his firm have handled many high profile and substantial injury cases including product liability, trucking accidents, escalator and elevator accidents, helicopter and plane accidents, boating accidents among others.

Mr. Penney is the host of *Radio Law Talk*, a radio show discussing the latest trending legal topics and news. Radio Law Talk is broadcast throughout many areas and can be found on SRN Radio networks. Frederick Penney as "has been featured in *Forbes, USA Today, Super Lawyers Magazine* among many other prestigious publications

ACCOLADES

- Lifetime Achievement Award America's Top 100 Attorneys
- Member Million Dollar Advocate Forum
- Member Multi-million Dollar Advocate Forum
- Sacramento Magazines Top Lawyers 2015-to present
- AVVO 10.0 Superb Rating for Personal Injury
- AVVO Client's Choice for Personal Injury
- AV Preeminent by Attorney Peers and by the Judiciary
- AV Preeminent
- RUE Ratings Best Attorneys of America Lifetime Rating
- Super Lawyers Rated Attorney
- Super Lawyer Northern California 2019

- www.penneylawyers.com/
- radiolawtalk.com/

Made in the USA
Las Vegas, NV
10 September 2022